HOW TO SURVIVE AS A
WORKING MOTHER

Lesley Garner graduated from Sussex University in English and European Studies in 1966. She has worked as a staff feature writer on the *Observer*, the *Sun* and *The Sunday Times*, travelled widely in Africa and lived in Ethiopia and Afghanistan. She now writes freelance for *Good Housekeeping* and *The Sunday Times*. Her books include *The NHS: your money or your life* and *The basic baby book*. She is married to a doctor and has two daughters.

How to Survive
as a Working Mother

LESLEY GARNER

Jill Norman

Jill Norman Ltd, 90 Great Russell Street, London WC1B 3PY

First published 1980
Copyright © Lesley Garner 1980

British Library Cataloguing in Publication Data

Garner, Lesley
    How to survive as a working mother.
    1. Mothers – Employment – Great Britain
    – Handbooks, manuals etc
    2. Women – Great Britain – Social
    conditions
    3. Mothers – Employment – Great Britain
    4. Great Britain – Social conditions –
    1945–
    I. Title
    301.41'2   HD6055

    ISBN 0–906908–04–3
    ISBN 0–906908–29–9 Pbk

Typeset by V & M Graphics Ltd, Aylesbury, Bucks.
Printed and bound in Great Britain at
The Pitman Press, Bath.

Contents

CONTENTS

Acknowledgements

If I make any one strong point in this book it is that no working mother can survive without help. The following people helped me to survive during the writing of this book, and their help was especially needed as it coincided with the birth and care of a second daughter, who shared my workroom and time until the book was finished and she was weaned. So I would like to thank my parents for extra help at the time of her birth and homecoming, and my husband Ken and elder daughter Harriet for their amazing tolerance and good humour. And a thank you to baby Rachel for being worth it.

Outside my own family I owe special thanks to *Woman's Own* and to Judith Gubbay in particular, for giving me access to the information they compiled for their campaign, 'Fair Deal for Mothers, Fair Play for Children'. They very kindly let me read the thousands of letters of support which their readers sent in to them at the launch of this campaign, and it is to these women that this book is in part dedicated. Each letter tells a life story and it brought home to me something that I knew already, though mainly through statistics, that the majority of working women in Britain lead tough and unrewarding lives. I would like to see these letters land on every MP's desk. In the meantime, I have quoted extensively from them because these working mothers tell their story better than I can. They deserve all the help we can give them.

The following people also gave me their time and expertise and experience. I would like to thank Carole Cowan, of Kindergartens for Commerce, Julie Kaufmann of Gingerbread, Peter Moss of the Thomas Coram Research Foundation, Jean Shapiro of *Good Housekeeping*'s Family Centre and Gillian Fairchild, also from *Good Housekeeping*. Thankyou to my agent Felicity Bryan who found me a copy of an excellent American book, *The Working Mother's Complete Handbook* by Gloria Norris and Jo Ann Miller, which I

ACKNOWLEDGEMENTS

found very helpful. I would like to thank my accountant, Peter Vaines, for answering my queries on tax and for directing me to his own very useful outline of the tax system in *The Writers' and Artists' Year Book*. I would specially like to thank my own personal safety net, Merrily Perks, whose loving care of my children helped me to get the work done. And, of course, I would like to thank all those working mothers, friends and acquaintances who took time to answer my questionnaire and to talk to me, not least of whom is my publisher, Jill Norman, a working mother herself.

1   Introduction – Why You Need This Book

A working mother friend of mine said *'I am sure your book will be very interesting but the trouble is that working mothers don't have time to read books.'* She was right, of course. I couldn't read them myself if that didn't happen to be the work for which I am paid. However, reading interesting books is one of those activities like visiting friends or making love to your husband that you haven't the energy for beforehand but you're glad you did when it's over.

You may be a working mother. You may be thinking about becoming a working mother. Or you may be married to one. If you are any of these things then I hope you will find this book helpful, constructive and cheering. I am a working mother too, so I know what a tightrope walk the whole business is, and I share the feelings of a mother who said to me *'There are days when I feel that none of it is working and I just want to go off to the North Pole and forget the whole thing.'* I am not so sure about the North Pole but the principle is sound.

We all read about women who juggle like virtuosi with large families of children, dynamic husbands, town house and country cottage, smart dinner parties and glittering careers and who practise yoga and Japanese flower arranging in their spare time. It may cheer you up to know that I did not meet anybody like that when I was writing this book. There were one or two who looked faintly superior from a distance, but from close-to they had the same haunted look in their eyes as the rest of us. They were aware of great gaps in their lives, of the thin thread with which the whole web was spun, of the vital importance of safety nets.

No working mother can survive without these safety nets, whether your particular insurance is your mother, a group of friendly neighbours, a highly paid nanny or, at worst, the welfare state. This book is a safety net too. If you're the kind of muddled, well-intentioned, slightly out-of-control, working mother that I am myself, then its very presence on your shelf will boost your morale. If you actually use it, then it will help you, but the very fact that you own it can make you feel more efficient, just as you feel a better cook for some good cookery books even if you live on Marks & Spencer steak pies. I don't expect you to follow all the advice in its pages. I don't follow it all myself, sound as it is.

And that's another characteristic of this book that I hope you will applaud. It's realistic. It's a 'how to' book, which acknowledges the way that people actually live, as well as the way that they *could* live if all were for the best in the best of all possible worlds. I may tell you how to retrain as an engineer but I point out that most women workers are crowded into part-time, badly paid jobs with no hope of promotion. I may tell you how to cook ahead but I have talked to mothers who forget to think about that night's dinner until the shops are about to shut. I may tell you how to fight for a better deal at work or how to set up a daycare centre, but I know that most working mothers are too tired to fight or to set up anything more complicated than a stiff drink at the end of the day. What I hope is that this book may present you with possibilities that you haven't thought of before. Lots of people don't fight and don't try to organise life to suit themselves because they don't know how to. I have tried to tell you how to, so at least you know that there are other ways of living.

'*Information*,' as Tom Stoppard wrote, '*is light*.' What I have done is to gather as much information as possible on every aspect of motherhood, work and working motherhood so that you have facts to help you make decisions and ammunition for stating your case. Life for families with working parents is only going to improve as more and more of them say what they want, and there *are* more and more of them. The number of working mothers in America has increased tenfold since the Second World War. Married women with children are the fastest growing sector of the working population throughout industrialised society. There are nearly four million working mothers in Britain, and nearly one million of them have children under five. It is these mothers with very young children who are the fastest expanding working group of all, and it is these mothers who have the worst problems when they try to find adequate care for their children so that they can go out to work.

It says something for the pressures that make women work that they are willing to tackle the awful child care problem in order to find and keep a job. No country in the industrialised world has a worse record than Britain for offering any kind of helping hand to the men and women who have to balance family responsibilities with a working life. This is partly because a disorganised but powerful lobby thinks that women with children should not leave the home to work at all. Patrick Jenkin, Tory Secretary of State for Social Services, said, '*If the Good Lord had intended us all having equal rights to go out to work and to behave equally you know he really wouldn't have created man and woman.*' But that attitude is as helpful and sensible as trying to put spilt milk back into the bottle.

I wrote this book because nothing, except severe recession, is going to stop more and more women working, whether they have children to care for or not. And the fact that they do work doesn't mean that they don't care for their children. We care a great deal more for our children than the politicians who accuse us of abandoning them and do nothing to lighten our load. I have talked to a great many working mothers and I haven't come across one that I envy. Even the most high-powered working mother needs a great deal of information to help her order her complicated life. I learnt a lot while I was researching this book, and I hope that however organised you may be, you will find something new and something useful in these pages. You have the right to work. You have the right to enjoy your children. And your children have the right to enjoy you. This book is meant to make it just a bit easier for you to achieve these rights. Good luck.

Part One
Working Mothers and Motherhood

2   Why Work?

Whatever their reasons for working I suspect that most mothers will sympathise with the harassed mother who wrote that the greatest bonus of going to an office was the bliss of being allowed to finish her sentences. 'Have you noticed how all mothers speak in a rush?' she said. 'That's because they know they're never going to get to the end of what they want to say without some child interrupting.' She also said that it would be nice to have a bath in peace, but I don't think she was able to do that at work. She worked because she needed the money, but she, and thousands like her, are proof that there are a variety of good reasons for going out to work and that most women, like most men, work for an inseparable mixture of all of them.

The most obvious reason of all is that the household needs the money. An article in Cosmopolitan smartly pointed out that a man's best hedge against inflation is a working wife. But what about a working mother's best hedge against inflation? In a growing number of cases the only investments against encroaching poverty are her own health, strength and working skills. At the rock bottom of the pile, hundreds of thousands of women in Britain work because they are either the sole breadwinner for their children or because their husband is so badly paid that the family could not survive on his income. The last census of England and Wales found 267,470 families in which the wife was the main breadwinner – two per cent of all married couples. Being the acknowledged breadwinner means that the woman herself has a full-time job or is looking for one and that her husband is either in part-time employment or is economically inactive. It does not even include families in which the husband is unemployed. So the number is actually much greater. Unemployed husbands who are actively looking for work do not appear in these statistics, but as the unemployment figures at the time of writing include 1,031,500 men, this makes a substantial difference. Add to that the fact that one family in nine in this country is headed by a single parent, usually a woman, who must work or claim supplementary benefit and that makes nearly 700,000 more women who are propelled irresistibly into seeking work in order to survive. So there we have around one million women who *must* work in order to provide the building bricks of the most basic standards of living – rent and rates, bread, heating, clothes.

Growing inperceptibly out of the substantial body of women who work for survival is an equally substantial body of women who work for money in order to improve their family's standard of living. Even here, there are women who work to relieve their family from poverty rather than to supply the annual holiday or a washing machine. There are 6 million low-paid workers in this country like this couple who work in one of the lowest-paid areas of all, the National Health Service. The wife is a state enrolled nurse working a thirty hour week on shift work in a recovery room of the hospital. She takes home £28 per week. Her husband works at another hospital as an orthopaedic appliance maker and his take-home pay from a forty hour week is £41.50. This couple never go out socially and they try to save £5 a week after they have paid the rent, the gas and electricity, their fares to work and food. '*I don't believe the majority of people can believe that there are such low-paid workers in this country,*' added the wife.

Another woman who wrote in to *Woman's Own* pointed out that her Chinese immigrant husband could only find low-paid work in a restaurant so that she, a teacher, was the major wage earner and paid over £30 of her salary each week to a babyminder. They had considered that the husband should give up work and stay at home to look after the baby. It would have made financial sense, but ironically the wife was concerned that he would be too isolated at home. At this level even very small sums of money can make all the difference to a family income. '*The amount by which I'm better off working than on social security is £15,*' wrote one mother. '*But that difference of £15 is vital between surviving and not. I grind my teeth behind the typewriter and know my daughter will never be this age again and I'm missing it.*'

And further up the scale are the thousands of couples who are trapped by the incoming tide of inflation. The most careful household budgets, the most economical housekeeping, the most virtuous thrift can be completely undermined by a jump in the mortgage rate, by rocketing price rises in supermarkets and garages. The couple who were going nicely become the couple who are struggling and then, suddenly, the couple who will go under unless some extra money comes into the family. If they take out the biggest mortgage that they can afford – traditional advice handed out to young couples – they are in danger of losing their house when the mortgage rate suddenly jumps a couple of per cent. The wife *must* work or all the saving is for nothing.

'*We don't want to rid ourselves of our children,*' said one. '*We want to be able to bring them up well and have a reasonable standard of living.*'

There is a growing, uncounted number of couples who either decide not to have children at all because it would mean the loss of the wife's income or who keep putting off the start of a family indefinitely until it becomes too late. '*I can't foresee a time when we will be able to have any,*' explains a young working wife, '*because my husband does not earn enough money to cover our large mortgage and all our outgoings. Therefore I will have to stay at work for at least another six years before we can even consider me giving up.*'

Mortgages may count as a necessity, but where does necessity end and luxury begin? Money means bread and marge and a roof over your head, but many women have found that it means a great many other things that they are unwilling to give up when they have children. Despite the wear and tear involved in juggling domestic work with outside responsibility, the effort is all worth while when a woman can dress her baby in clothes that she bought herself out of her own income, or can take the children out on treats, or pay for the family holiday. The husband may provide the mortgage but the wife can furnish the home.

'*The number of things you can do diminishes if you give up one salary,*' said a doctor who had provided a country cottage for her family; but for most people it is the difference between buying better clothes or eating more meat. The danger comes when an income which was once regarded as an extra becomes a necessity. We are entering the era of a two-income life style, when both halves of the couple *must* work in order to make life worth living.

Money is inextricably involved with another increasingly important reason for working – independence. '*I did some part-time work,*' said a mother recalling her early married days, '*and it was the first time in my life that I was making money. It was a revelation to me and once I'd had it I wasn't going to lose it. I think being paid is essential. It's not having to ask for money which, however willingly it is given, is a hand-out.'*

'*I've always worked,'* said the mother of two children who runs her own publicity company from home. '*It's not for the money, not primarily, but because I'm doing a commercial job with a market value I want to get the rate for the job.'* She works for identity – what some call independence and some call self-esteem. It's that feeling of being human that can vanish after the birth of the first baby if you're used to independent living, even if that baby is the thing you wanted most in life.

'*I thought about it when I'd had my eldest daughter for a few months. Those first few months or so when I realised I could never again just go out of the house and never again just think of myself were quite traumatic. I was knocked out by being a Mum. I wanted her very badly, but I was quite old, in my thirties, I'd had this business of having lived all my life quite selfishly. Now I was turning myself inside out.'*

What that mother wanted to do – and did – was join the human race again. She wanted to feel useful to people beyond the walls of her home. She was experiencing what many mothers experience for the first time when they have babies, that muffled feeling of looking at the rest of humanity through glass, of watching the world go by without them. The power that drives women like this back to work is not so much the idea of fulfilment, it is more the idea of wanting to belong again, wanting to renew one's membership of the working world.

'*It gives me an important part of my identity to know that I'm needed and one of the team,'* says one, '*and that people are counting on me to do my job. I think to be a productive, competitive worker is something we all need. I've never heard anyone talk about this, but in all the jobs I've held since school, I've got a deep satisfaction from being a part of a team of people working together, being part of the work force. I think it's a basic instinct of humans – to work co-operatively, to know you can pull your weight with the rest.'*

What is peculiar to industrialised society is the idea that, by becoming a mother, you have to step off the economic treadmill, that motherhood and belonging to the workforce are incompatible. Before the industrial revolution a mother was a cog in the economic machine just as much as her husband was. She made much of the equipment needed in the household. She grew food and preserved it. She made clothes and bedspreads and rugs. She was a producer. With the industrial revolution and the specialisation of work and its removal to the factory an women lost this usefulness, this knowledge that they co contribute to the economic well-being of their family. Shopping for loss leaders in the supermarket is no substitute for creating wealth in a family. Home and work became separated from each other. No wonder that women feel lost when they become cut off from the main stream.

'*However small a cog*,' said a mother who built up a career in publishing after she had her two children, '*I was still part of the main wheel*.' Usefulness is therapeutic. Any doctor can tell you that. much. As Diana Davenport, author of *One Parent Families* says succinctly, '*The actuality of working, quite apart from the necessity of gathering in loot, instills confidence no end. Work helps you meet people, exercises the brain, takes us out of ourselves.*'

A study carried out among the women of Bermondsey in south east London noted that women who went out to work seemed to have started a new lease of life. These women did not think that they were neglecting their family by going out to work – although a strong family network helped them a great deal. They thought that by working they were caring for their family better. They gave the sociologists who were engaged in studying them the impression that they were '*energetic and resourceful individuals living the busiest of lives*'. They would have sympathised with the *Woman's Own* reader who '*managed to complete a six month job with a great deal of help from friends looking after my eldest until I got home from work. It was hard work but I felt a new person socialising again, giving me something to look forward to and running a home at the same time.*'

'*I like the feeling that you're getting so much into your life*,' said another. '*I like the idea that life is an adventure.*'

What is interesting is that this therapeutic effect of work outside the home is not tied to rewarding professional work – the kind of work that goes with ideas of a 'career' and 'self-fulfilment'. It is to be found as a side-effect of any job that gets a woman, even temporarily, back into the adult world and viewed as an individual, not as a mother. That's why Mary Kenny, in her book *Woman × Two* pointed out that lots of women were perfectly happy earning a modest wage doing '*a nice little job – many people want a simple, unworrying job, a nice time and a bit of cash*'.

They do not want to be in the position of the *Woman's Own* reader who gave up work for her first baby and found herself cut adrift. 'Here I sit at 33 with five O'levels and a career in accounts work behind me unable to be of any use to any one outside my own family. All I want is a little help to retain my individuality and expand my horizons without my children suffering.'

This woman, like millions of others, had another very good reason for wanting to work after she had children as well – habit. It is all too easy to forget, in the heat of the debate over whether mothers should go out to work or not, that most mothers are workers before they become mothers. They are educated in schools to think of what work they want to do and then, invariably, they go freely into the working world before they marry. It is uncommon to give up work when you marry these days, so the birth of a first child is usually the first time any young mother has been on her own at home. No wonder so many mothers suffer from withdrawal symptoms, or find it hard to imagine giving up work in the first place.

'I've always worked,' explained a journalist who has three daughters. 'I just can't imagine not working. I'd probably beat my children to death or something if I weren't working. I was back working within a month of having my first child and I was doing half days – rushing back home to breast feed. I'd be unendurable if I didn't work.'

'I gave up work automatically when Rachel was born,' said another. 'That was what was done then and I was a person who always did what was done. I hadn't thought about my life at all. I thought marriage was a full-time job and I was glad to stop work. Slowly I became aware it wasn't a full-time job.'

When Woman's Own conducted a survey into working mothers they found that over half of the mothers who work have been bored and lonely at home and desperately need a break. Four out of five of the working mothers they questioned said they would still like to go out to work even if they did not need the money. The sheer loneliness and depression that can come with being confined in the walls of one room or home all day have had millions of words spent on them. I do not propose to add to them. If you have not experienced this loneliness you cannot begin to imagine what it is like, and if you have experienced it then you do not need me to tell you how negative, how entirely destructive it is. The facts about working women are not cheering. They do not, on the whole, do fascinating and rewarding jobs, they do not, on the whole, earn good salaries. So, as Barbara Toner points out in her book, *Double Shift*, it must be a measure of desperation of home-bound mothers that so many want to work despite the dreary prospects.

'*It seems to me you lose your identity when you leave a job to get married and have a family. They only think you need cleaning jobs because that is all you know, but we know other things as well. Cleaning jobs are what you want to get away from,*' said one. '*I am middle-aged and very much need companionship because I am very lonely all day at home,*' wrote another. '*Also I could do with the extra cash. I haven't been out to work for some years now and would so much like to widen my outlook. I get so depressed at times.*'

A graduate wife with two young sons who now works as a secretary said that she worked for the money, '*but I do like getting out of the house as well. I got married straight out of university. I'd got one of those useless general degrees that don't qualify you for anything. I was very fed up and paranoid staying at home and I had friends in similar situations.*'

But there are more sound reasons for mothers to keep working than a desperate flight from the prison of home. However overwhelming and isolating the early years of motherhood may be, they are over quite soon and mothers are suddenly faced with an empty future for which they are quite unprepared. Like the middle-aged woman I quoted earlier, they find themselves abandoned by their children, beached on their own hearth rug, with rusty work experience, no qualifications and few prospects of a reasonable job. However precarious the balance between children and work, more and more women are realising that it makes sense to keep some kind of a grip on the working world so that the inevitable step back after the years of intensive child care is made easier. By the time most women have finished with motherhood, they still have half their working life before them. They should beware of getting to that awful stage where they need the children more than the children need them. If they do not look this far ahead they may find themselves in the traumatic situation of needing to join the working world again and being completely unprepared for it, like the divorced wives quoted by Brenda Maddox in *The Observer*.

'*Many of the women who are getting divorced at about fifty,*' said one perceptively, '*Are choosing liberation without being trained for it. They are anachronisms. Succeeding generations of wives will have kept a career going which could fill the gap for us now but many in my age group did not return to work when the children reached school age. So we have to job hunt as well.*

13

Not an easy task when, depressed and unskilled, we view the unemployment problem.'

'*It seems small wonder that my marriage broke down,*' said another. '*I knew nothing about anything and hadn't bothered to find out. I had never earned my own living. I no longer regret becoming divorced. What I do regret is not having taking the trouble to learn both before and during my marriage, all that I have learnt since it came to an end.*'

Few women today can afford the luxury of abandoning work completely. But the fact that the working world seems to demand them full-time or not at all is just one more problem facing women with families. The world of work does not make it easy for women with children to treat it as a casual acquaintance. Most mothers given a chance, would probably like to work part-time while their children were small. This would provide them with all the benefits they expect from a paid job – some money, some self-respect, some independence, some time outside the home, few child care problems, a chance to come to their children refreshed and energised rather than worn out by a day's labours or by the monotony of home. But part-time work, as I shall show later, lies mainly in the least attractive areas of employment. And full-time work makes no concessions to the families of its employees, male or female. The world of work is simply not designed for families. It does not want to know about them either.

There may be ways in which family life and work could adapt to acknowledge each other's demands, and I will be looking at those too. But until they are put into practice the majority of mothers who must work will continue to suffer a dual load of strain and responsibility. This stress has created two further minority groups, sad ones. There are working women who would love to be mothers but daren't and there are mothers who would love to work but can't. This second group have largely had to abandon the idea of working for a number of reasons. The *Woman's Own* survey found that 80% of the non-working mothers they questioned said they would like to work, if possible, but 52% of them had been unable to find anyone suitable to look after their children. Amongst those mothers who do stay home with their children, there must be a sad number who have lost all sense of self-worth, both as mothers and as people – like this unhappy *Woman's Own* reader who is probably passing on her own sense of hopelessness to her daughter.

'*Both my husband and myself feel I'm being wasted sitting at home all day with my three year old when I could be doing a useful and worthwhile job. I care for my child and want only the best for her but why should my whole life be given away to produce yet another woman who will in time have her own children to stay at home for? What a waste!*'

When the conflict between the desire for work and the demand of motherhood produce such despair and confusion, the most urgent question to ask is what has gone wrong with motherhood? It is supposed to be the peak of feminine achievement and fulfilment, the most creative role open to any human being. So why do all these women find that they cannot live by motherhood alone?

3   Good Mothers, Bad Mothers and the Rest of Us

WANTED

'Worker to look after one adult male, children and run family home. Applicant must be 100% reliable and prepared to commit her/him self to the job in hand. Applicant must be kind, loving, cheerful, very patient, adaptable and have a strong sense of humour. Good health and physical stamina highly desirable. Suitable applicant must be able to function on minimal, broken sleep in the early stages. Organisational ability a great help but not essential. Personal qualities more important than professional qualifications. Hours of work are 24 hours a day, 7 days a week, 52 weeks a year. Hours of work diminish with age but responsibilities and commitment continue until death do them part. No guarantee of time off. No guarantee of sick leave. No guarantee of pension. Prestige negligible. For right applicant rewards are enormous though intangible. Salary and expenses nil.'

If you have never seen an advertisement like this in the newspaper it is because the perfect parent substitute is not to be had on the open market. This book is about mothers as people with occupations other than motherhood and the lengths to which they must go in order to balance their needs with the needs of their families. But it is not a book which disregards the importance of unalloyed motherhood. If motherhood were not important there would not be so much fuss made about any attempt to dilute it. If it were not so responsible and time-consuming there would not be a 'working mother problem' at all. This book is about and for mothers who also work for money in the outside world but it knows that every mother already has a full-time job. Motherhood *is* work. It is not a second-rate, small-time occupation that intelligent women are right to abandon as soon as they get the chance. It is a full-time, fascinating, demanding, absorbing job in its own right.

It is a job which has no pay, no agreed conditions of employment. It is a job without holidays, without break, without

– for more time than you thought possible – any decent sleep. It is a job that will take more out of you than you imagined you had in you and will give you more than you ever expected you had to give. It is a job that will have you sobbing damply into the nappies and a job that will make you laugh more than you have laughed since you were a child yourself. It is also the only crucially responsible job that lets you learn as you go along. In fact there is really no other way to do your apprenticeship. However rotten a parent you sometimes think you are, you have to be very rotten indeed before anyone else will be considered an adequate substitute by your particular family.

Full-time motherhood is the most interesting, enjoyable, boring, rewarding, demanding, maddening, delightful, monotonous, time-consuming, relentless, exhausting and inexhaustible work open to any human being. It is work that few beginners take on in full consciousness of the commitment. Very few first-time mothers really know what they are letting themselves in for. You may consciously decide to become pregnant. You may consciously rearrange your life to make room for a baby. You might know quite a lot about babies before you start. You may even know some personally. But not until you actually hold your own, unique, idiosyncratic, small person in your arms do you realise with every corner of your being, whether joyfully or in despair, the absoluteness of the commitment you have taken on. You have a responsibility, and it is that responsibility that makes a mother out of you, whether or not you stay with your children 24 hours a day.

What makes irresponsible, cheerful, liberated girls take on a life time responsibility of parenthood? Women who were very articulate when I asked them why they worked, became monosyllabic when I asked them why they had children. The woman who said simply, '*I want children*', was more lucid than most. It is really only since the advent of the Pill that the question has had any point or meaning. 'A woman's choice' is a very modern concept. Ours is the first generation which has really had to exercise a choice in the matter of having children.

Sociologists Robert and Rhona Rapoport have come up with a little list of reasons – having children makes people feel complete (biology again), it makes them immortal, it demonstrates their sense of altruism and responsibility, it increases the sources of love

17

open to them, it gives the parents some power and influence over other human beings, it is fun, it is creative. And, I would add, in most societies it is economically useful. In the pre-industrial west and in peasant societies all over the world children offer help with the family work and insurance against their parents' old age. They also give pleasure and prestige to grandparents. I remember thinking, when I first became pregnant, that for the first time in my life I was going to do something that would be approved of by absolutely everybody in my family. It is not a motive to be overlooked.

You may wonder why I have been going on about mothers and not about those more fashionable creatures, parents. Although I believe strongly that the future survival of the family and the individuals in it rests squarely on the shoulders of fathers as well as mothers, there is still a universal acceptance of the fact that mothers bear the main burden of responsibility for the care of their children. It is the mother who has to decide whether to work or not, the mother who must make arrangements for alternative care of her children and the mother to whom the children usually turn. If it were not so, I would not have to write a book about how to cope with all these demands.

The irony is that this splendid, omnipotent figure does not enjoy prestige and glamour and importance in relationship to all the effort put in. Because motherhood, extraordinary as it is, is so universal, so very *ordinary*, women who choose to be full-time mothers get little or no credit from the rest of us. Mothers are taken for granted by their own children, by their husbands and by society at large. It is hardly surprising that when they threaten to upset the applecart, politicians and all the other indirect and direct beneficiaries of selfless motherhood become alarmed. Drawing their feet back from the horrid sight of so many turning worms, they proclaim the final argument: 'Children need their mothers.'

This is where the writer breaks down in the hopeless search for an alternative word. Children need a lot of things and their mothers may be among them but what do we mean by saying that they need their mothers? What, in other words, is a mother? Do children need the person who biologically gave birth to them? Not necessarily. Do children need someone to love them? Certainly, but it need not be their mother. Do children need somebody who is going to provide a secure and loving home, a haven to return to, a shoulder to lean on? Yes, they do, but even that need not be their mother.

There has been a great deal written by earnest and well-meaning persons about what children need. When they are babies and toddlers they need a very great concentration of physical care, an enormous amount of loving attention, a constant watchfulness and responsiveness, a pleasant environment, games and laughs and cuddles and certainty. Whatever age they are, they need physical and emotional security, real interest in their doings and depressions and enthusiams, warmth and food and shelter. Most of all the child needs, as child expert Elizabeth Newson put it succinctly, '*to know that to someone it matters more than other children, that someone will go to unreasonable lengths for its sake*'. Or as I heard an American psychologist say endearingly in a television programme, '*Someone's just got to be crazy about that kid.*' However good the substitute care provided for her children, no working mother should ever forget that her children are people who have rights, the first and foremost of which is this right to the passionate commitment and unconditional love of at least one adult human being. They have a right, when necessary, to come first.

But these needs and rights which belong to your child do not mean that you have to feel vital and irreplaceable the whole time. I personally believe that children have an equally important need to have a variety of friendly people to inject the sheer otherness and difference of life into their daily experience. Even if I did not work I would want my small children to spend time outside the home and to mix with different people in order to stir a little richness into their lives. Children need champions, but grannies and grandads, aunts and uncles, cousins and brothers and sisters can be as effective champions as their mothers and fathers and can help to introduce them gradually into a wider and less friendly world.

The idea that children must spend the first years of their life alone in the intensive care of their mothers is a freakish one. It is not the norm, either from our own past or in other societies. It is certainly not a realistic preparation for life. In more simple, non-industrial communities the mother is supported by the rest of her family. Children accept it as normal to see their mother too occupied with work to give them her full attention; and they accept it as normal that other people are reliably there to entertain

19

them and care for them. But since the death of the family economic unit, too many other members of the family go out to work beyond the family or the village to give support to the mother or time to the child. This intensive little mother and child unit has been isolated from the rest of daily life and the result has not been a great improvement in the quality of motherhood or a happy life for the child.

So the fact that a mother may want to leave her child in the temporary company and care of other people may not mean that she is a bad mother. As long as she is considering the needs of her child when she does it, she probably thinks she is being a good mother. In wanting to enliven her life and expand her child's horizons a little, she is certainly being a normal mother. Experts are very careful not to use the word 'good' or 'bad' in describing mothers, but ordinary people are not so inhibited. Most of the women I talked to had a very clear idea of what a 'good' mother was and they were doing their best to be one despite their commitment to outside work.

One divorced mother with three teenage children at first resented the fact that life had not allowed her to be a good mother like her own, a woman who had raised 11 children and whose life was centred entirely on the home. But she had found out early in life that 'good' mothering had more to it than undiluted domesticity.

'When the children were young and I had to work it was a time of constant guilt. I felt very guilty because of not being the mother I thought I'd be. I'm a very maternal person from a big family and I felt small children needed their Mum there all the time. I didn't like leaving them, I wanted to be there playing with them and taking them to the park. So there was a conflict between my desire to be a mother and my desire to pursue my own dignity. But looking back as I grew a little older I realised that my mother had no knowledge of the outside world and I resented her. She didn't have anything to tell me about what women did, about what opportunities might be open to me. I just thought I would have to do the same as her, get married and have children. My children have a much more realistic idea of the world than I did. I know now that I'm a very good mother. My children have plenty of my time. I'll drop everything to talk to them. If I'm washing clothes at one in the morning because I've spent the evening talking to them, so be it. My kids are normal, fairly independent children.'

Working women who have to crowd their lives with

responsibility have learnt one invaluable fact, that quality in dealings with other people counts far more than quantity, and that being with your children all the time is not nearly as important as being available to them at the times when they really need you.

'*I had an incredibly good mother,*' explained a magazine editor. '*She told me that she spent a lot of time with me, but you know, it was no such thing. It was war time and she was terribly gay and social, always jetting about. I've thought about it since and it boiled down to certain things. One is that she was always there when we were ill. Then she took a keen interest in what we did at school. She never missed a school play or anything like that, so I try to do that. I join in the girls' school activities as much as I can and when I get in from work I grab a drink and rush upstairs and read stories with them and so on.*'

What these two women are consciously doing is setting out to be what they see as good mothers and it has nothing to do with sitting at home with their children. It is a more adventurous concept than that. They do their best to be available at times when their children really need them, and as well as giving their children 'quality' care, they also offer them a link to a richer life, a picture of a woman who has self-respect, who is active and useful in her own right, a model of someone that the children can be interested in and inspired by.

They don't think that motherhood has to be a 24 hour a day job, although it is, and always will be, a 24 hour a day responsibility. This idea that motherhood, in order to be of any use at all, has to be full-time, is at the heart of the attack on working mothers. The child psychologist, John Bowlby, stirred up the worst of it by his post-war studies on the effects of maternal deprivation. Being apart from your mother when you were young was, he concluded, a bad thing. His conclusions have been much disputed since, but even Bowlby said the quality, not quantity was what counted. '*The provision of a proper diet,*' he pointed out, '*calls for more than calories and vitamins. We need to enjoy our food if it is to do us good. In the same way, the provision of mothering cannot be considered in hours per day, but only in terms of the enjoyment of each other's company which mother and child obtains.*'

Where the 'children need their mothers' argument falls down is that there is more and more evidence that when children get nothing *but* their mothers, both parties suffer. One study of mothers in six different cultures found that mothers who spent a high proportion of their time with their children were actually less loving and more irrationally irritated with their children than mothers whose time with their children was diluted. A wider study of 45 different cultures found that there was a clear correlation between lack of physical affection, even child abuse, and mothers isolated with young children.

'*All these men who talk about the glory of motherhood,*' complained an American mother, '*should spend a few rainy days with a houseful of kids watching the television, asking for a drink of water two hundred times a day, interrupting whatever you're doing, breaking things, asking you questions – and try to keep their sanity. Try as you will, you're not the mother you want to be, you turn into this snarling, screaming Mommy. You look in vain for some effect you're having on them and all you can see is whining and power struggles.*'

Another mother who started off wanting to be perfect found that after six months alone with her baby, she was depressed, tearful, timid and lonely and, of course, guilty for being so feeble. '*I couldn't understand how anyone could love the baby the way I did and still hate the routine.*'

She, and all isolated young mothers, have been trapped by the modern ideal of separate, domestic motherhood. An American sociologist, Jessie Bernard puts the case against it very strongly. '*The way we institutionalise motherhood in our society – assigning sole responsibility for child care to the mother, cutting her off from the easy help of others in an isolated household, requiring round-the-clock tender loving care and making such her exclusive activity is not only new and unique but not even good for women or for children. It may in fact be the worst – it is as though we had selected the worst aspect of all the ways in which motherhood is structured around the world and combined them to produce our current design.*'

It's the sole responsibility that's so crushing. Full-time mothers are the victims of the theory that this early time alone with their child is the make or break period in its life, that she alone can cause or prevent lifelong anxieties and neurosis, make it secure or insecure, loving or deprived. The burden is just too much to bear. It's nonsense, and one can only hope that fashions in child care make a swing that relieves some of this pressure on the mother. By seeking to get back into the human race while their children are still small, more and more mothers are helping to scotch this theory and are, if they did but know it, trying to revert to a more traditional way of balancing working and family life.

In peasant societies, children are absorbed without stress into the business of growing up and becoming members of the whole community. They help in the everyday tasks of providing food and shelter and bringing up yet more children. All these tasks and all these people are confined to a comparatively small geographical area so that this gregarious, communal way of life is entirely practical, as well as friendly. Life in industrialised societies is much more complex. In order to survive each family has to produce enough wealth to purchase a huge array of specialised services and commodities – electricity, gas, petrol, water, foods, clothing, radios and televisions and newspapers, toys, entertainment and cars. They have to pay taxes in order to provide the services of the welfare state – health care, education and defence.

The production of this kind of wealth, unlike the simple production of a village is the enemy of family life. Even where only one parent goes out to work the family is split up, and the sheer expense of life increasingly means that both parents must work to maintain a reasonable standard of living. Old people remain economically active so that the grandmothers and aunts who might have helped with the children are not there, or may be far away as job mobility splits families still further. The growth of transport and commuting means that the members of the family may be as much as fifty miles apart during the day.

All these things are normal facts of late twentieth century life but officialdom like to pretend that these dramatic and revolutionary changes have not occurred. They expect families to behave in a pre-industrial manner, and the one person on whom the burden of keeping up standards falls most heavily – and with least support – is the mother. If she goes out to work she gets blame and no help. If she stays at home to look after the children she gets no thanks and no help. 'Children need their mothers,' say the politicians and the employers as if that absolves the rest of the community from any responsiblity to help.

But I think that the importance of the parent is more complicated and has more faces than this black-and-white view implies. Childminders, nursery nurses, teachers, nannies and grannies and sisters and cousins and aunts, all the range of parent substitutes and parent helpers who look after our children in our absence, can only operate effectively if we, the parents (biological

23

or otherwise) have laid an unbreachable ground of love and security at home. It is our job to provide this solid foundation of support and care, and if we do, there is room for a good deal of architectural variety in between. How we provide it is a matter for each individual family, but if we have done our best to provide it then we have done our essential task and we can – all things being equal – step into the working world quite free of that debilitating, universal maternal infection, guilt.

4   Guilt and How to Live With It

Guilt and motherhood go together like bread and butter. And like butter, guilt has a nasty habit of spreading. Mothers not only feel guilty in themselves but can cause guilt in other people. They may pass a little surplus guilt on to their families at the end of a particularly harassing day, or they may remain sweet for years and suddenly spill the stuff in all directions just as the menopause hits them and they suffer the pangs of too much strain, self-sacrifice and lost opportunities. These distressing facts apply to full-time, stay-at-home mothers just as much as mothers who try to do paid work outside the home.

Even full-time mothers who enjoy their lives are sometimes made to feel guilty that they are so satisfied with their lot. They secretly wonder what sort of feeble creature they must be to stay at home with their children while other women rush about running businesses single-handed, organising immaculate homes, preparing sophisticated dinner parties and patting their radiant children on the head at regular intervals. '*I'm only a housewife, I'm afraid*,' says the stay-at-home wife with an apologetic smile and she spreads her guilt back at the working mother by joining the '*I don't know what she has children for if she's only going to dump them in the nursery*' school of thought.

Working mothers are very vulnerable to jibes like this, especially on days when the system does not seem to be working as well as it might. Under the carapace of every career woman is a heart that bleeds at the accusation of neglecting its family. The '*What did you have children for if you're not going to bring them up yourself?*' lobby is a strong one, particularly in Britain, and lines itself firmly up behind the trenches of inertia which surround government policy – or non-policy – on anything to do with the problems of working mothers and their children. The underlying principle is that officialdom must not provide any help because to do so would only encourage them. It is reinforced by what one might call the theological argument, the '*If God had wanted women to go out to work he wouldn't have made them mothers*' line.

Politicians have a great deal to do with reinforcing or lessening the guilt felt by working mothers. Simon Yudkin and Anthea Holme in their study, *Working Mothers and Their Children*, point out that '*this somewhat guilty attitude appears to be new though by now it is widespread and deep. During the last war there was little evidence of it . . . Helped by the provision of numerous day nurseries, many mothers took full-time jobs and left their children in day nurseries from 7 a.m. until 7 p.m.*' But we no longer have a war effort to support, so mothers who wish to leave their children in order to go out to work can safely be thought of as selfish and irresponsible.

The undeniable guilt felt occasionally by most working mothers hangs over four main problem areas.

1. You think the children are suffering.
2. You think your husband is suffering (this usually happens after you've served shepherd's pie three days running or fallen asleep when he was trying to make love to you).
3. Your work is suffering.
4. Nobody is actually suffering except you, either because you think somebody *ought* to be or because it has been suggested to you that they are.

Within this framework mothers feel guilty about all kinds of absurd little things. Guilt can be triggered by unwashed laundry, un-ironed shirts, holes in his socks, forgetting to buy the children new shoes, buying a birthday cake in a shop, being too tired to change anyone's sheets. Where children are concerned, all working mothers are an open wound, vulnerable to any attack. The sharpest pangs of guilt undoubtedly occur when children are ill. '*Illness is the worst thing,*' said the mother of two little girls. '*Last winter we had endless illness and I had to leave the little one vomiting into the sink and it nearly killed me.*'

'*I don't believe that the pre-school period is worse,*' said another. '*I worry more about having children at school and the fact that they get home and I'm not there. The awful things are more likely to happen when they are out and about. There was one ghastly time when I was in a meeting and they got hold of me and said my daughter had gone through a plate-glass door. The au pair we had then was wonderful and she'd taken her straight to hospital. I did feel frightful about that. Actually I felt guilty all the time from the beginning.*'

Even when we lived abroad I felt guilty about working because ex-patriate wives simply didn't work. They left children to go to lunch parties and bridge but that was different. Work was thought selfish. I argue with myself. I convince myself that it's not damaging as long as someone you really trust is with them. My feelings about it are all a reflection of my children's state. If they stand howling at the door then it's hard, but they do that anyway – they do that if you're on the phone.'

School children are also vulnerable to too much organisation and zeal on the part of their mothers like the ever-guilty mother who managed to send her five, seven and nine year old children off to school early because she had to rush off to work and got them there an hour before the gates opened – in January, in the snow, with no overcoats and gloves. Her children have never let her forget it. This inability to slot the different areas of life together smoothly – and most especially the inability to arrange satisfactory child care – is at the root of all the guilt and strain. *'I know it's terrible,'* wrote one *Woman's Own* reader, *'but I find myself wishing my daughter's life away by thinking it will be good when she's old enough to go home alone, and I still won't be there with a nice warm fire and tea ready like I used to have and would love to be able to do.'*

Children who make a fuss about being left alone can make mothers feel terribly guilty even when they suspect, or know, that the child is testing them out. A doctor who had two babies and only worked part-time found even the part-time work hard to start with. *'The first child was very nervy and cuddly and when he's upset he really turns it on. It was very hard at first. I used to feel terrible and go off to work very tense and unhappy but it was very manipulative screaming. It stopped as soon as I'd closed the door.'*

In an effort to quash all this guilt, working mothers may be tempted to spoil and over-compensate their children. If this means spending more concentrated time with their children when they are at home, then both parents and children benefit, but it is dangerous when it means extra treats, even sweets and presents. All the mothers agree that children soon learn to recognise the signs of guilt on their mother's face and to take advantage of the potential weakness. The most lasting answer to suppressing or vanquishing this guilt is to look hard at proven facts about families where mothers work, and to knock prejudice over the head with them. The greatest cause of guilt among working mothers is the wide-spread myth that working women are at the source of all

27

breakdown in a family. We come back to John Bowlby and his studies on deprived children – not only deprived but very disturbed, orphaned and institutionalised children after the Second World War. He concluded from studying these children, that separation from a permanent mother or mother substitute was highly damaging to the child's mental and emotional health and could affect the rest of his life. But this fairly unexceptionable conclusion cannot be extended to children from stable homes whose mothers leave them with good caretakers to go to work outside the home regularly. The child is only separated from his mother temporarily and predictably. The child knows that the mother always comes back.

Numerous studies that have investigated the problem of separation of mother and child since Bowlby's original studies have produced *no evidence* that partial separation of a child with a good minder or a good nursery causes any damage to the child. These studies have come up with no differences between children who spent part of the day away from their mothers and those who spent all day with their mothers. Where there are differences these are linked to the mother's personality and not to whether she worked or not. The problem comes in separating the mother's personality problems from her need to go out to work. In other words a mother might become disturbed because she is depressed at home. In taking a job to get out of the home she would hand her child over into someone else's care, but any unhappiness in the child is likely to be due to the fact that his mother was already disturbed, not because he was in someone else's care. You could say that the fact that the mother was getting out might improve her temper and his happiness even though mother and child were apart a great deal of the day.

Studies done on slightly older children of working mothers have found that any differences in sociability and educational standards were mostly in favour of children of working mothers, and that the children's teachers regarded the primary school children of working mothers as being more than averagely intelligent and mature. Another study, carried out by Barbara Wootton into criminal behaviour in adolescents found that the *quality* of care and supervision was more important than whether the mother worked or not. It was quite possible for the mother to be at home all the time without keeping any control over her child and if this was so, he was more likely to become delinquent than the well-supervised child of a working mother. In fact the father plays a much greater role than the mother in determining whether or not a child becomes a delinquent. Judith Hann quotes a study in her book *But What Shall We Do With the Children?* which found that 98% of a cross-section of juvenile offenders were without a father or father-substitute, but only 17% of them had no mother. So much for the evil effects of a mother working.

If you still think your children might be suffering as a result of your work, don't rely on theory. Look at your child. Train yourself to be hypersensitive to any sign of stress or strain and tackle it before it becomes serious. Are your children extra clingy? Over-tired and tearful? Do they seem to be having more nightmares and disturbed sleep than usual? Are they aggressive or destructive? Are they eating badly or eating too much? Have they become withdrawn and timid? The first aid treatment for this kind of disturbance is time. You may have to give something up – in which case turn to pages 33–37 of this chapter which deal with priorities. But in the meantime, cheer yourself up by thinking of the very considerable benefits which a family can get from having a working mother.

Something in your circumstances should be improved by your working or there is no point in doing it. It may be that you are better off/more stimulated/more relaxed/more fulfilled. It may be that the family finances are greatly improved so everyone benefits from a higher standard of living. It may be that you are more fun for everyone to have around. It may be that the interest of your job rubs off directly on your family – you might have perks they can enjoy too, like cheap travel, cut-price food, free theatre tickets, interesting people to know. It may be that having a break from home makes you that much nicer to everyone in it when you are there. If you are not much better off financially and hag-ridden into the bargain, and if your children are genuinely unhappy, then you should look seriously at the situation and see if there could be a better solution.

But most mothers who can make the juggling act work at all agree that there are lots of benefits, both for them and their families. We have already seen that the children of working mothers can be marginally brighter and more aware at school. Another side-effect is that they can also be more ambitious. They have seen, through your example, that people can get up and do something with their life, and if you are the mother of daughters this example is more than a bonus, it is a duty. Career expert Ruth Miller reports that girls tend to take their mother's lead in choosing a career, or in planning out a life of motherhood and work. If they have stay-at-home, unambitious mothers they tend to be unaware that life has anything more to offer. If they have get-up-and-go mothers then they can see for themselves that life is full of choice and excitement. Once children are old enough to be aware of what their mothers do for a living, working mothers win a lot of respect for themselves from their children. The teenage daughters of working mothers are most likely to nominate their mothers as the person they most admire.

An American study came up with even more interesting results. The effect of having a working mother in the family tilted the whole balance of sexual attitudes. What happened was that the children of working mothers had a higher estimation of their *own* sex as a result – girls saw their mothers are more competent and effective, and boys saw their fathers as more warm and expressive, the result perhaps, of the man having to take on more of the caring side of family life when both parents worked. The daughters of working mothers were asked to describe what activities they thought women liked or disliked doing and they seemed to think that working women enjoyed everything more than housebound women – household tasks as well as paid work – which says something for the tonic effect of work. Nor did the children of working mothers lose out on their mother's attention. Mothers who stayed at home claimed to spend six or more hours a day with their children as compared with four hours for the children of working mothers. But by the time the children reached adolescence there was no difference between the two groups.

If you take quality into account some people claim that a confident, working woman who feels what the French call 'well in her skin' spends more positive time with her children than a full-time mother. This is perhaps borne out by another study which found that the full-time mother who stayed at home out of the dry feeling of duty, not pleasure, had the lowest scores of all.

A woman executive in one study said, '*When the children were very little they would rather have had me at home but when they got to about nine or ten they were proud of me. I think I possibly make a better mother to older children. My own mother was a very motherly mother. But when I was about eleven and started asking lots of questions to which they didn't know the answers, my parents felt threatened. Now when my son knows more than I do, I'm glad. I have an assured position.'*

A lot of women report a growing sense of responsibility in their children as a bonus of working, which may bear out one point of view that children – like adults – thrive on a certain amount of stress and rise to the challenge given a certain amount of encouragement.

'As for the children,' said one, a publisher, *'I think it makes them resourceful and independent. They're used to the idea of doing things for themselves, to getting themselves organised in the morning. They're used to the idea of women being independent and doing things. The games they play are based on it. Oddly enough, mothers and fathers they play the conventional way, but they play going to work at publishing, they play making books and bookselling and going to book fairs and offices. The other thing I'm pleased about is that they're used to the idea of not being looked after by only one person, they respond to everyone.'*

'The girls absolutely accept it,' said another mother with three daughters. *'They're terribly balanced and normal. My eldest daughter and friend have already plotted their careers. They're going to go to University. Then they're going to share a flat and write novels and have several children. Because they've both got working mothers they're both very mature.'*

'They're interested in what I do,' said a third. *'It relieves them of all sorts of pressures too once they're establishing their own life. There's no great weight of "I'm sacrificing everything for you."'*

Working mothers can congratulate themselves on the fact that with the control of their own lives more firmly in their own hands they have less need to control their children's. Being their own woman, they can sit back and allow their children to be themselves too.

But even women who work hard on all fronts to produce balanced, healthy, happy children and competent work can be undermined by a snide remark from a far from well-meaning observer. With the support of the people closest to us – our husbands, our own parents – we can be proud of ourselves. Without it we can be reduced to a shivering heap of guilt. Beware the grandmother who sets herself up as your children's champion. Beware the non-working mother who says *'if you wanted to work, why did you have children?'* Beware the half-hearted husband who rings you up during the day to say that the baby has been crying for you, and thus destroys your nerve and concentration for the rest of the day. Beware men.

'*My male colleagues made me feel guilty because all their wives stayed at home and looked after their babies,*' said one, and a single mother who had to work and was therefore comparatively guilt free was still undermined by her friends' husbands.

'*Nobody tries to make me feel guilty although I have a friend who's divorced and she stays at home with her own kids, but she gets so much maintenance that I feel she's justifying her own situation when she digs at me. The major thing is men – they see it as me pursuing a role. They don't see me as a breadwinner. I've got friends down the road and the husband was sitting in the garden drinking beer so I stopped on my way to work and I said "it's all right for some", or something like that. And he said he was on holiday and he said "it's different for me, I'm the breadwinner. I have responsibilities." I said. "Yes, but so am I." And he ruffled my hair and he said, "Ah, yes, but you don't understand. It's not the same thing." Boyfriends say, when I have to say I can't see them because I've got so much to do, "Well, why don't you give up work?" It's terribly irritating. There's this assumption that women who work are there because of a whim, or because they are hard career women.*'

The fact is that when anything goes wrong in your family, you, the unnatural working mother, will be the natural lightning conductor of blame. Whatever niggling doubts you may have had about your situation will be seized on by your family doctor, your children's teachers, or figures in authority who will try to make you feel as though you are the last person to put your children first, as happened to this secretary whose son was sick at the school Christmas party.

'*He's always sick when he's excited, but the school went berserk when they couldn't get hold of me at home. The school gave me the impression that everyone cared more about my son than I do. My husband was readily available – he works nearby – but they seemed to think that this was a terrible arrangement. And when my son was going through a difficult, testing-me-out phase and didn't like going home from school on his own, one of the neighbours collared me and told me I wasn't fit to be a mother. I must admit that hurt.*'

Authority figures – especially schools – can often be won round if you explain your situation to them in advance. One single parent who did this at her son's school put her case so well that when the schools went on strike the headmaster looked after all the children of one parent families himself.

With guilt coming at them from so many fruitful sources (not least of which is themselves) working mothers need to know how to defeat the insidious enemy. Guilt is a completely counter-productive emotion that causes anxiety, fatigue, depression, sleeplessness and procrastination. The fact that you feel guilty about your husband's meagre diet or un-ironed laundry does not get him better fed or better clothed. The fact that you feel guilty about missing your children's bedtime is no use to them unless you either come home earlier or put them to bed later. The fact that you feel guilty about anything is more likely to make you behave like a wet hen than a sensible human being.

Guilt is the source of all kinds of flap and muddle and if you are to survive at all you must learn how to kick it under the carpet. The first rule for handling guilt is this. If you really and truly have something to be guilty about, stop it. If you suspect that your child is being beaten by her childminder, if you know that you are doing shoddy work, if you think you are driving your husband into the arms of another woman (or the local pub) then stop. Reassess the situation. The fact that women with small children have a very broken record of staying in one job for any length of time is an indicator of how difficult it can be to make the mixture work in this period of your children's lives. A very great number of women who are not absolutely desperate for the money and not highly motivated to push their own careers do give up at this point to concentrate their energies on their families. There are times in every working mother's life when this may be the wisest course.

The second rule is to be clear about priorities. If you have decided to carry on working there will be many times when something in your life has to give. If you know in advance what can be shelved then you are not likely to be caught in so much of a muddle. Most of the stress, unhappiness and breakdown in life comes from having a mind and energies that are torn in two or more directions. People who achieve what they set out to achieve are always single-minded, if not all the time, then at least while they tackle what needs to be done. If you can concentrate on each task or person or situation as you cope with it then you are a formidable source. If you are not a millionaire or a Nobel Prize winner already then you have the makings of one. The rest of us, unfortunately, are all too apt to listen absent-mindedly to our children because we are thinking what to have for dinner tonight, to make a typing error because we realise it is nearly time to collect our child from the minder's and we might miss the bus, to snap at our husband because we've just realised the baby is completely out of clean nappies, or to burn the boiling potatoes because we've just remembered an important phone call we should have made.

The truth with which you must learn to live is that combining the running of a household, the care and company and love and entertainment of children and husband with a full-time paid job is excruciatingly hard work. Doctor Miriam Stoppard once described the life of a working mother as 'sacrificial'. I wasn't one at the time and I thought she was exaggerating, but I know now that she was right. All too often it is the mother who ends up on the altar waiting to have her throat cut – or wishing she could do it herself. Working motherhood is not a tenet of faith, it is a constant daily reappraisal. Many a mother in her moments of exhaustion and despair wonders whether or not to devote all her time and energy to her family since they seem to consume it anyway. She should realise that in many ways the greatest danger is to herself. When it comes to sorting out priorities, it is only enlightened self-interest for a mother to put her own sanity first and that may mean dropping something else.

'*What I used to feel,*' said a mother who learnt the hard way, '*was that I wanted to do the things I wanted to do thoroughly. I'm a perfectionist and I've never been allowed to perfect anything. But I adjusted to it. I think I've developed a terrific capacity for self-tolerance. You have to say "Sorry, I can't do it, because I can't do everything." I felt I had to be good and best and perfect so I have suffered from that. Then I realised that I would never have the kind of house my friends had where people could walk in any time and it would be lovely. My house is a tip. It comes last and I've learnt to live with it. My priorities are children, work, house.*'

Without priorities women often report on missing some good things in life which they would rather not have missed. The most easily spoilt of these – and most important – is a closer relationship with a child. When the topic of working motherhood comes up people always talk about the children missing out on a closeness with their mothers, but the truth is that women need their young children as much as their children need them.

'*As for having time with the children,*' says one, '*I often think that I haven't seen them. I mind not seeing them in the evening and so do they. There's a definite publishers' thing of having drinks together at 5.30 and I didn't join in that because of the children, but not doing that has had a negative effect on my work. In an ideal world I would have enjoyed greatly having more time off when they were babies. I was breast feeding them both but it dried up. One I fed for six weeks and the other for two months and yes, I did mind that. My biggest regret is that I miss out on so much with the girls.*'

Another mother described coming home in the evening and hearing her daughter and the nanny having a lovely, giggly time from which she felt entirely excluded. In an ideal world she would have had another child and spent more time with this one but she gave her high-powered job priority, right or wrong. Suddenly realising that you have missed something that you did not want to miss is one sign of lack of priorities. Confusion and muddle is another.

'*I always pull myself back when I can feel myself snapping or nagging,*' explained a hard-pressed single parent. '*It's a sign of undefined priorities. This background moan that makes the atmosphere* bleaagh – *it means I'm not convinced about my leadership in the house. I make myself go back and state what I want clearly. I know things are bad when I can't wake up in the morning or if I feel permanently harassed. The danger signs with the children are when they keep bursting into tears, and they're not feeling well. Then I'll drop everything and sit down and talk. I watch for that. If things are going badly I think it's fair enough to spoil them outrageously, to go home early to get them a good meal and bring them a hot drink in bed.*'

Knowing when to drop everything is the art which can make a guilt-free mother of you. It means you have come to terms with the different elements in your life, that you have got them in perspective and, as far as you can, are doing your best by them within your limitations and in balance with each other. Once you have decided to shelve the problem, however temporarily, *stop worrying about it.* When the pressure mounts up on you, stop and ask yourself these simple questions. Is there anything I can do about this particular problem at this particular time? Which of these problems *can* I do something about at this particular time? Once you have chosen your problem, concentrate on it *to the exclusion of all the others.* If you cannot tackle the problem then do not think about it until you can. That way madness lies.

The unfairness of working motherhood is that you may be faced with making this kind of decision not once but many times in the course of a day. Whether you work in the home or outside it, whether your children are tiny or at school, whether your husband gives you a lot of help or none, there will be some areas in your life that don't bear inspection. It cheered me enormously, as I talked to other working mothers, to realise that I was not the only one whose social life was non-existent. I no longer feel so guilty about letting friendships slide since I learnt that social life is one of the first things to go in a frantic effort to cram everything in. I also learnt that the world is full of neglected husbands, though most wives do feel guilty about that and make an effort to put something else to one side to make it up to them.

'*My husband goes grumpy and declines if he thinks he's not getting enough attention,*' said one wife, *and I sometimes feel great strain. Then I get scatty and very tense and bad-tempered. If this happens I try to clear a few days. But we all get on a lot better because I'm not there all the time.*'

In fact husbands seem to be a tremendous source of guilt, whether they demand attention or give it. Splendid, supportive, Husband-of-the-Year type husbands who do their share around the house and listen to their wife's hard-day-at-the-office stories generate just as much, if not more, guilt than husbands who snarl about missing shirt buttons and go off to the pub for a decent meal. Of course they may just be going to get out of the house which, as far as I can see, is right at the bottom of most working mothers' priorities.

'*I did want a beautiful life,*' said one sadly. '*I've always had this image of candlelit dinners and everyone serene, but I've never quite managed that. It worries me that the house has never been properly decorated and that the garden has gone to seed.*'

If the state of your house worries you a lot, you may prefer to move it to the top of your list, like the mothers who can not learn to let go of all their traditional tasks. '*I tried to do most things,*' said a secretary who spends ten hours a day away from her home. '*I'm very possessive about chores. I have an overwhelming conscience about what I do and I'd rather be tired and guilt-free.*'

If you would rather be guilt-free and not tired either, then work out your own set of priorities. If something has to give, make sure that it isn't you. You may have to live with a layer of dust over everything or turn down a promotion or get a job nearer home or spend time with your children when you could be going out to see your friends or an evening in with your husband instead of learning yoga. Hobbies, like housework, usually come well below family and work. '*When I fill in forms*,' said an overworked mother, '*and I get to the bit where it says "hobbies", I just sit and stare at it.*'

Sitting and staring may be a luxury too, but if you think that a bit of sitting and staring is essential to your survival then do it – don't feel guilty about it. You have to be quite tough and competent not to suffer from the guilt trap and it is quite likely that if you are that hard, you will have organised your situation to be as guilt-free as possible anyway. You will have convinced yourself that your job is essential to your own and your family's well-being, that nobody suffers from it, that your children are thriving and then – like the majority of people – you will simply be getting on with it. The rest of this book is devoted to telling you about practical ways in which you could lighten your own load, either by arranging better child care, training for a more interesting job or persuading other people to back you up.

5   Getting a Quart into a Pint Pot

'*We struggle on,*' wrote a journalist working mother in *The Guardian,* '*trying to pack one week's work into every day, encouraged by the sort of magazines we write for to be the perfect lover for our husband, the perfect mother for our children, the perfect wife for our house and a more than perfect worker in our chosen career. Of course we fail. We fall into bed too weary for more than a chaste kiss, we nag our children, we don't find time even to banish the cobwebs and sometimes we put in a less than perfect performance when out at work.*'

'*Life's too short to stuff a mushroom,*' said Shirley Conran succinctly. And I say, '*Show me a working mother who's a perfectionist and I'll show her the way to the psychiatric ward.*' Something, in every working mother's life, has to give. It is the working mother's number one task to make sure that it isn't her. What you allow to slide to the floor in your own overcrowded life is a matter of little choice guided by a lot of desperation. It may be cooking gourmet dinners or ironing your husband's shirts or reading the newspapers, but go it must. Priorities may be the key to avoiding guilt. They are also the key to surviving through the week. All too often the working mother gets to bedtime to find that her day has somehow been organised for her. A phone call hasn't been made, a wall hasn't been papered, the husband hasn't been kissed or the cat fed. Along the hectic path of her life other tasks presented themselves more urgently and emergencies came first.

If this describes your life and if you have a nagging sense that you are missing out on something good because your energy goes on innumerable less important things, then it is time to make space for a thorough look at where your time and energy are going. Making this first step towards a newer, brighter, more streamlined life is a very cheering pastime in its own right, even if it is also the last step. It is no accident that lists are the mark of an organised woman. Crossing items off a list certainly makes you feel good, but so does making the list in the first place. It represents the imposition of order on the chaos all around you. Even if you do not follow it, it is reassuring to have it to hand as a sign that, whatever a muddle your life is in, at least your brain is tidy. Or, as one working mother said, '*I don't have a mind anymore, I have a notebook.*'

Once you take stock of your day-to-day life in this way, I have found from all the working mothers I talked to that stress and strain focus on certain easily recognisable areas. These are the mad scramble each morning, the problem of time wasted in travelling and lunch hours, the when-to-do-the-shopping-and-housework problem, the what-to-have-for-dinner (and who) problem and the when-do-I-get-time-for-myself-and-the-family problem. The solution is organisation though not all hot organisational tips work for all women. One woman's bulk buy is another woman's storage problem. One woman's cook-ahead meal is another woman's mouldy and forgotten pan of mince, but certain general principles hold.

'*If the wife was to make a success of going out to work,*' said the social workers of the Bermondsey study, '*she needed the intelligence to plan a routine and the character to stick to it.*' As an illustration of this organised industry, they looked at the 15 hour day of one typical Bermondsey wife who juggled a morning and an evening job with a husband and four children to look after. She rose at 7 a.m. to prepare the breakfast and get her children off to school and work and to tidy up her own house. Between 8.15 and 10.15 she worked nearby and between 10.15 and 11.00 she shopped for food. By 11.30 she was back home doing the washing and preparing lunch for her family. After she had served and washed up the lunch and dealt with the dry washing she went out at 3.45 p.m. to shop for tea and came home again to prepare and serve it. At 5.00 she went out to work her evening shift and returned home just before 10.00 to swop baby-sitting duties with her husband before he went off to start his night shift. There is not much room in that timetable for fun and games and most working mothers will recognise the early start.

Getting up early – or earlier – is one unpleasant but guaranteed way to get more into the day – unless you collapse earlier at the end of it as a result. '*There is no work like morning work,*' sang Mrs Beeton, '*particularly household tasks, and those we take early in the day, fresh from a night's rest and a good breakfast, are trifles "light as air" in comparison with the same dragged or hurried through later.*' One mother I talked to made a habit of getting up at 5 a.m. once a week and luxuriating in the unaccustomed peace and quiet. Other mothers, less extreme, use early morning time to talk to their children – to have a friendly breakfast with a toddler or to lie in an early bath and talk to their daughters as they get ready for school. A third shares the getting of breakfast with her sons and a fourth makes the breakfast and packs school lunches before throwing her clothes on and leaving the unwashed dishes. Before dashing off to work she parades her children in front of her to see what they might need during the day – dinner money, a note for school – before running to get her train.

That journey to work is deeply resented by any working mother who has more than a short walk or bus ride. '*Pure dross,*' is how one mother describes the commuting train which eats three hours out of her day and more than one mother counts her lunch hour as an undiluted waste of time. The only way in which working mothers seem able to turn this time to advantage is to treat it as personal unwinding time – difficult to do on a crowded commuter train, but a journalist who spends an hour on the London to Brighton train twice a day as part of her 12 hour shift uses it as relaxation. '*I work on the morning train and on the evening train I unwind. It's a different world on the train. Nobody knows who anybody is once they leave the train, but we're all friendly while we're on it and it's a tremendous relief to get on and find someone has saved your seat and bought your drink already.*'

If you can find a job near to home it seems that it saves time, money and nervous energy, as well as meaning that you are near to hand if any family emergency crops up. Commuting mothers are accutely aware of the troubles that might be occurring long distance and become adept at coping with emergencies over the telephone.

The much resented lunch hour can, of course, be used to do the shopping. Full-time working mothers tend to use up valuable weekend family time by doing the weekly shop. If they are not as organised as this then they will warm to the honest mother who admits to a daily five o'clock panic over what to have for supper and ends up buying baked beans at the corner shop on her way home. Keeping a running list of household needs on a pin board or black board is one very effective way of making sure you don't run out of urgent items out of shopping hours. Super-efficient mothers don't let themselves get caught like this. Depending on the grade of their efficiency and the state of their bank balance they manage to stock up weekly, quarterly or even yearly. One highly efficient woman who uses an account at Harrods as her personal safety net says that she runs her home just as she runs her office *'so that things don't break down. I do a twice yearly bulk buy of all the standard household things – toothpaste, loo paper, cleaners and so on. I never shop daily, only once a week. Then Sunday morning or Monday evening I do some cooking ahead. I buy fresh things, a roast or something for the first couple of days after I've been shopping. Then I make a couple of casseroles. I've got a reasonable freezer in the top of my fridge. Then Friday night is left-over night or we go out.'*

If you want to save time – and money wasted in inevitable supermarket impulse buys – you can shop by phone and by post. Otherwise you can make your shopping so boring and routine that it becomes an automatic process like the couple who whisk round Waitrose every Saturday morning with two large trollies. *'He gets all the store stuff like toilet rolls, soap and I get all the rest. We buy the same things each time. It's a routine. We spend £40 (for a family of seven) and that's it. I then get the meat from a local butcher and put everything in the fridge-freezer.'*

Organised shopping inevitably means organised eating, because in order to shop ahead you must plan your menus ahead. Not necessarily three months ahead like one mythically efficient working mother – but even two days ahead lifts you out of what Katherine Whitehorn calls the *'Oh God, dinner'* brigade. As she points out in *How to Survive in the Kitchen*, a useful book for hate-to-cook working mothers, the *'Oh God, dinner,'* brigade who ought to benefit most from the cook-ahead, freezer-filling approach to life and food, rarely do because by the time they remember that dinner is looming up again it is too late to thaw anything out.

Menu planning is just too much for some working mothers like this one. *'At 5 p.m. I think "panic, panic" what am I going to give them for dinner and where do I get it? All this thing about planning a week's meals I just can't do. The more I buy at the weekend the more they eat so it's still all gone by Monday. I'm always either over- or under-buying, forgetting what we've run out of. I cook rice with mushrooms or I buy cold chicken and have it with pasta, or I get mince for shepherd's pie. My standbys are eggs, cheese and home made soup. Whatever else I forget you can always make a meal out of them.'* And another mother finds cooking ahead greatly over-rated as a time saver. *'Theoretically I try to cook on Sundays for a whole week but it tends to take up Sunday if I do. I cook up mince in various ways and I make flans and pizzas ahead and I do use a lot of convenience foods.'*

As a compromise between a weekly hamper from Fortnums and a delicious freezer full of gourmet food, and the other approach which means you end up with a take-away from the fish and chip shop, I do recommend the doubling-up system by which you cook double amounts and freeze the left-overs. I did it once and I felt very virtuous and it was lovely to have a spare meal lurking in the fridge. I mean to do it again one day.

Along with the what-to-have-for-dinner goes the who-to-have-for-dinner problem – not a cannibal's delight, but the question of whether you invite friends round or not. You can clear your social decks once or twice a year in splendour, like the wife who makes the point of throwing one huge, grand supper party and putting her family through hell while she does it. Or you can exhaust yourself putting on regular dinner parties. Or, as most working mothers seem to do, you can find out who your real friends are by refusing to entertain and discovering which of your acquaintances still keep in touch despite the bread and cheese. Unless cooking is one of your relaxations, this course of action has a great deal to recommend it.

If you are one of those people who find cooking and housework both therapeutic and soothing, time spent in peeling potatoes or doing ironing can legitimately count as time spent on yourself. One working mother sends her children out on Saturdays, puts on some music and potters about with the Hoover. *'I find it gives me time to calm down,'* she explained. Another enjoys the time spent in preparing food, and Mary Kenny recommends the more nurturing household tasks such as tending plants and making bread as excellent therapy for the harassed working mother. Housework treated as a way of clearing a space around you and ordering your life can make you feel more refreshed, not less.

But if you cannot blend two areas of your life in this way then you may be among those working mothers who need to set aside a clearly defined area of your time for yourself and your family. One mother insists on her weekly yoga class, come what may. Another family refuse all social invitations at the weekend and lavish all their time and attention on their two daughters. A third family make a treat out of Saturday tea, and spread a blanket on the floor before the television and stuff themselves with cakes while watching 'Doctor Who'. Nothing at all is allowed to interfere with these private pleasures as parents and children get back in touch with themselves and with each other.

With forethought, the surroundings of daily life can be better organised to make sure that family life is protected and that neither work nor the unproductive demands of housework take priority over the emotional needs of parents and children. The pressures of work can actually have a salutory effect on the running of a house. An American study has shown that while stay-at-home housewives spend as much time doing housework as they did forty years ago, despite all the new labour-saving devices, working women have brought their housekeeping hours right down. Is your house a slave driver or a machine for living in? Is it suitable for a working family with other demands on their time than elegant living and constant housework? Is it child proof? Are you wasting time and energy protecting your possessions from your children? Have you made sure that paint and floors are easily washable, valuable belongings out of reach, carpets and soft furnishings difficult to stain and easy to clean? And have you chosen a neighbourhood which provides a safe and welcoming background for children to grow up in? Can your children have a degree of independence there? Are there safe places to play and friends to play with, a short journey to school and good neighbours to keep an eye on things when you are not there?

If you have organised your external circumstances to allow as much leeway as possible for your busy life, have you looked at the way you run it? There are enough books on the market to help you, from Mrs Beeton to *Superwoman*, and they all contain good, sound sense which not even the most high-powered mothers should scorn. Like other successful gamblers every working mother needs a system and the essence of that system is back-up. Behind every successful working mother is help, in one form or another, whether it is a book, a kitchen full of labour-saving devices, a splendid husband and a team of children or a genuine, old-fashioned treasure.

It is very popular to denigrate the labour-saving device in all its guises as a snare and a delusion. Articles frequently appear in women's magazines to the effect that machines will end up running you if you are not careful, and that they are guaranteed to break down when you need them most. I would take this view with a pinch of salt. Part of its popularity is that it is easier to write amusing articles about machines breaking down than it is to write paeons of praise about the wonders of washing machines. Personally I could not live without my washing machine now that I have it. I *have* lived with servants during the times I have spent abroad, and I would rather have machines any time.

Contrary to the whimsical journalist's view, machines are far less trouble than people. They don't hang about the house making you feel guilty if you don't have enough work to keep them going or if you decide to have an afternoon nap. They don't have difficult wives or strong political opinions or days off to attend family funerals. And any fit of temperament by a machine can be sorted out by a swift kick or a visit to the mechanic, whereas temperament on the part of human help can poison the atmosphere for days.

Which domestic appliances you use to lighten your load is largely a matter of personal life style and house room. Everyone who has a freezer swears by one, whether they use it as a store cupboard or belong to the cook-ahead brigade. Nobody who has a washing machine would be without one, especially if they have babies or small children in the house, and although you hear a great many arguments against dishwashers, you never hear them from the people who own one. Dishwashers kill two birds with one stone in that owners of dishwashers not only have clean dishes but very tidy kitchens too. Food processors only earn their keep if you do a lot of cooking and have somewhere to keep them ready to use.

Even if you can not afford domestic aids at this level, there are simple pieces of equipment which can ease the household load. A wipe-clean noteboard in the kitchen has made a great deal of difference in my household. As soon as we notice that the washing up liquid is low we write it down and save the cursing that accompanies that last useless squirt of bubbles from the empty bottle. Another disorganised mother I know swears by a notebook in which she writes down each task as it occurs to her.

One source of assistance is free and always ready to hand – your family. If you are going out to bring in the bread, your husband will have to play his part in running a house, and your children, however young, are never too young to help or to take in the idea that they are part of a working team in which everyone does his or her share. In fact little children are only too eager to help, even when this help actually creates more work for you. In order for this help to be willingly given, a great deal depends on the kind of boss you are around the home. It helps if you make it clear what you expect of each person and to what standard you expect it. It helps if you don't nag. It helps if you are properly appreciative of everybody's efforts – after all, one of the great complaints that women traditionally have about housework is that nobody ever notices when it has been done. You should notice. And you should be firm. If a task is not done, let everyone see the consequences.

'I say what I want clearly,' says one mother of three teenagers. *'I say "the breakfast washing up must be gone before you get an evening meal," and I come back that evening and if it isn't done, I stick to it. I go to my room, even if it means cooking a meal at eleven that night when they've finally got round to it. My kids clean up the kitchen regularly, though they usually "forget" about the saucepans. I never, ever, touch their rooms even if it means you can't open the door. My younger son is splendid. He'll cook, sew, do his own washing. Apart from him I have one male chauvenist pig and one liberated female who thinks housework is beneath her.'* Lots of mothers of teenage children admit to leaving their rooms alone and to confining their interference to tossing clean sheets at them once a week. Even a mother who guards her household tasks jealously, admits to seeing a beneficial effect on her two young sons when they have to pull their weight. *'Sometimes I think my sons have got more responsible, they appear to be more part of the household than before. They can get shopping on their own and so on.'*

One rule for getting help out of your family is never to let anyone get away with the *'I'll do it but I'll do it in my own good time'* attitude. Husbands are particularly adroit at this, if they help at all. Some husbands are magnificent helpers, others have a long way to go.

'Roger is the original useless male,' says one loving wife. *'He was brought up to do nothing and his mother picked up after him. I'm training him to realise that when he does housework he's not "lending a hand" he's "doing his share".'*

'My husband,' says another, *'is of that generation of Englishmen who were born not to help. He is very charming but absolutely idle. I honestly think that if I earned a great deal more money than he did he would be happy to retire. Three or four years ago I realised that things would never be better and I realised I could never divorce him because the children adore him, it would be too much for them. So I live with it.'*

And a third wife made the telling point that when her husband went away, he left everything to her, whereas if she had to go away for any reason she had to leave a freezer full of food, a list of where to find anything and a complete safety structure for every eventuality. If you cannot rely on your family to help you then you should consider paying for help. You need not be letting yourself in for a houseful of staff that one working mother maintains on her salary – a living-in housekeeper, a daily help, a nanny and a secretary – but you could possibly afford to pay a local school girl to do your Saturday shopping or to baby-sit. Or if your children refuse to co-operate any other way you could pay them for their assistance. Whichever path you choose, don't be the kind of mother who will not let go of any part of her responsibilities. Instead be the kind of mother quoted in an American handbook who said, '*I've gotten so far as being able to say "the hell with it, so I'll live with a messy home", what I'm beginning to learn now is that I've a right to a clean home but it doesn't have to be me that makes it clean.*'

Part Two
Working Mothers and their Children

6   Working Through Pregnancy

Once upon a time if you became pregnant while you held a job you automatically lost it, and that time was not so long ago. Now you have the right to continue working until they're calling for the ambulance, if that is what you want, and to have your job back again. Once upon a time if you became pregnant you automatically assumed that this was the end, temporary or not, of your working life whether or not you were sacked. Your girl friends got excited and you left work early in a shower of presents and retired to your home and nursery. Some people still do that, but more and more women are working through pregnancy even if they decide not to return to work after they have had the baby.

There are some good reasons to continue to work during your pregnancy even if you do not need the money. Pregnancy can be very boring. As you grow heavier and more cumbersome you won't feel like rushing about anywhere and the time will go more and more slowly as your time gets nearer and nearer. It helps to have an occupation. Of course, a lot depends on how you personally feel while you are pregnant. If you have a very nauseous early pregnancy you may not feel like working at all. On the other hand, work helps to take your mind off your own maternal condition. It is all too easy to become very inward looking and self-obsessed as your stomach rises and rises to blot out the outside world.

Once the early three months of pregnancy are over – and you should certainly guard against too much strain and stress in this period – the middle three months usually go swimmingly and it is only as your pregnancy draws to a close that it becomes burdensome. Doctors usually advise people to carry on working because it provides pregnant women with something to do. Your job is not a threat to a healthy pregnancy unless you do something obviously dangerous like sky-diving. Even ballet dancers and other athletes often work through a great part of their pregnancy and it is worth remembering the following little anecdote from an American obstetrician who told his patients that they could do anything, absolutely anything when they were pregnant except play tennis. He mentioned this to a colleague who said that he thought tennis was perfectly safe and that personally, he always told his patients they could do anything except ride horses. The first doctor discovered his colleague could not stand horse riding and he admitted that he himself was quite hopeless at tennis. After that both doctors told their patients they could do anything they liked.

If you have decided to stay at work until the baby is nearly due, you need to know the laws protecting pregnant women at work, and you also need to know what benefits the state allows pregnant women and when and where to claim them. Your most immediate concern is to know where you stand with your employer, particularly if you want to return to work once your baby is born. I have summarised the Employment Protection Act as it affects pregnant women, but I recommend anyone who wants to to into this area in more detail to get hold of all the relevant government leaflets which I list at the end of the book and to read one or all of the very useful handbooks on women's rights which I also list.

WORKING THROUGH PREGNANCY – THE EMPLOYMENT PROTECTION ACT

The Employment Protection Act extends its protection to you if you have been working for the same employer for two years before the beginning of the eleventh week before the baby is due. It is of no help to the many women who have been with their employer for less than two years or to part-time workers who work 16 hours or less each week. 821,000 women fall into this category. It also indirectly penalises women who find it difficult to stay in the same job for long because of the problem they have in making arrangements for their children. If you do work less than 16 hours a week you may be eligible for job protection if you have been with the same employer for five years and if you work at least eight hours a week.

The rights which you have under the law are:

1. Dismissal from your job purely or mainly on grounds of

pregnancy is now unfair dismissal and you have right of appeal to an industrial tribunal.

2. You have the right to be reinstated in your job for up to 29 weeks after the birth of your baby.

Pregnancy and Unfair Dismissal

Your employer has no right to sack you because you are pregnant. If you have been working for him for at least six months and he does sack you when you are pregnant, this counts as unfair dismissal. There are two exceptions to this rule. One is if he feels that your pregnancy has made you incapable of doing the job properly – it could involve heavy lifting or you might be a strip-tease artist or a jockey. The other is in the rare case that it is illegal and dangerous for your job to be done by a pregnant woman – working with X-rays, for example. But even if one or other of these cases applies, he is still obliged to offer you a suitable alternative job if he has one. If you think that he had a suitable alternative and did not offer it to you before sacking you then you can claim unfair dismissal. If you think you have been unfairly dismissed you have the right to take your case to an industrial tribunal. You have up to three months to make your claim and if you win you could be entitled to compensation as well as your legal rights.

Reinstatement After Maternity Leave

To qualify for getting your job back after your maternity leave you must:

1. Have been working for your employer for at least two years at the beginning of the eleventh week before the baby is due.

2. Have carried on working up until the beginning of the eleventh week before the week in which the baby is due.

3. Have informed your employer that you intend to exercise your right to return to work (a) at least three weeks before you leave work; (b) at least one week before you intend returning to work.

4. Provide your employer with a certificate signed by your doctor or midwife giving the estimated date of the baby's birth.

51

If you have been fairly dismissed before the eleventh week before the expected date of birth for one of the special reasons already given, you are still entitled to get your job back, whether or not you accepted alternative employment during the remainder of your pregnancy.

According to the law, the job to which you return must be the same job you were doing before *according to your contract of employment*. You would be well advised to check the wording of your contract and clear up any possible misunderstandings in advance. For example, if you work in a large office or store, your contract may simply describe you as secretary, clerical worker, sales assistant. You do not want to come back to selling underwear if your job used to be selling televisions. You might not want to work in a canteen if you used to be working for the advertising director. If any pay rises were awarded in your absence you are entitled to benefit from them. If your employer refuses to give them to you then you can take him to the industrial tribunal. If, having returned to your job, you want to have another baby, you do not have to wait for a further two years in order to benefit under the Employment Protection Act.

The statutory limit for returning to work under the Act is 29 weeks from the birth of your baby. If you do not return to work after this time is up you forfeit your job, except under certain special circumstances.

1. You are allowed a four week extension if you are ill.

2. Your employer can delay your return to work for up to four weeks after the statutory 29 if he warns you before the end of the twenty-ninth week.

3. You can delay your return to work in the case of strikes or any other industrial disruption.

These are your legal rights and they sound quite good. Unfortunately there are a few flies in the ointment as you may discover for yourselves if you get pregnant and want to return to work. One of the worst problems is that the right to return to work is not supported by any provision of child care. I look at this problem in detail in the next chapter because good quality child care is the corner-stone and foundation of successful working motherhood. The right to return to work is absolutely meaningless unless the mother can find somebody who will take good care of her baby. At the moment this poses an insoluble problem to most mothers of tiny children. What this means is that the woman who most needs to return to work has the worst deal, because her need for the job is so great that she has to settle for inadequate childminding. The result is an unhappy child, a distracted mother and her job inefficiently done. Nobody wins.

Another problem is that not everybody benefits under this law. I have already pointed out that many part-time workers are exempt. You also get no protection if you are self-employed, if you are a member of the police or armed forces, a woman whose sole employer is her husband (surely you could come to a satisfactory arrangement here?) or a master or crew member engaged in share fishing paid solely by a share of the catch!

A Department of Employment study into the way in which maternity protection actually works found some flaws. In the case of reinstatement, they found that employers have the problem of not really knowing whether the employee is going to come back. It is not uncommon for a woman to say she will return in order to keep her options open, or to mean to return but then find herself unable to find someone to take care of her baby and have to abandon the struggle. Small firms have a particular problem in putting the woman back in her original job, if they have had to replace her during her absence. The Government is considering requiring the pregnant employee to provide a written notification of her intention to return at least 28 days before she means to come back to work and not seven days as at present. She should also provide an additional notification in writing not later than six weeks after the birth of her baby if she means to come back to work. If she fails to do any of these things she may forfeit her right to return. Although I have outlined the provisions of the law it is quite likely that your individual employer may have a more generous arrangement. Your trade union will advise you here.

How to Complain to an Industrial Tribunal

You can complain to an industrial tribunal if you think you were unfairly dismissed during pregnancy, if your employer refuses to pay you the maternity pay to which you are entitled, of if your employer refuses to let you return to work after the birth of the baby.

Your local Job Centre or Employment Office or Unemployment Benefit Office will provide you with the proper application form, Form IT1. if you are not sure where to find these offices, look them up in the phone book under Department of Employment. Fill the form in and send it to The Central Office of Industrial Tribunals, at the address on the form.

You must make your complaint in the three months following:

1. the date on which your notice expires or the date on which you were given notice;
2. the last day in which you were paid if you are appealing against a failure to give you maternity pay;
3. the date when you intended to go back to work if your employer refuses to have you back.

If you have any problems in making your claim or dealing with the industrial tribunal, ask for help from your trade union, or your local Citizens Advice Bureau who will help you find a solicitor who is part of the Legal Aid scheme. It will be good for your morale to seek help from these sources in any case, whether or not you feel quite confident about pressing your case single-handed.

MATERNITY RIGHTS AND BENEFITS

There are several different kinds of maternity benefits, some of which come directly from National Insurance and some of which are related to your employment. Entitlement to these rights is not as simple as you might think because they are dependent on your own or your husband's National Insurance contribution during the previous year. It is as well to go to your local office of The Department of Health and Social Security as soon as you know that you are pregnant and read the relevant leaflets. If you are unsure whether you are entitled to a particular benefit or not the staff will be able to look at your case with you. The relevant leaflet which explains maternity benefits is DHSS leaflet NI17A entitled *Maternity Benefits*. There is also a pamphlet produced by the Department of Employment called *Employment Rights for the Expectant Mother*.

NATIONAL INSURANCE MATERNITY BENEFITS

The Maternity Grant

This is a lump sum of £25 payable to you if you or your husband have payed Class 1, Class 2 or Class 3 National Insurance contributions on at least 25 times the lower weekly earnings limit of £26.50. You must have paid or been credited with the same amount of Class 1, Class 2 or Class 3 contributions in the tax year which ended the April *before* the calendar year in which your baby is due. In other words, if your baby is due in February 1980 the tax year which counts is the tax year ended April 1979. You can claim the maternity grant if your baby is still-born provided the pregnancy lasted at least 28 weeks. If you have more than one baby at a time, you get an extra £25 for each baby that survives. In other words, twins are worth £50. You claim the maternity grant on claim form BM4 and it can be claimed at any time from 14 weeks before the baby is due to three months after it is born.

Maternity Allowance

The maternity allowance is a weekly allowance claimable on your own National Insurance payments only. You must have paid Class 1 contributions on earnings of at least 25 times the lower weekly earnings limit of £26.50 and you must have paid or have been credited with Class 1 contributions on earnings equal to 50 times the lower earnings limit, or 50 Class 2 contributions in the tax year which ended the April before the calendar year in which the first payment of the allowance is due. Maternity allowance currently stands at £18.50 per week and it is payable for 18 weeks. You claim the maternity allowance on claim form BM4 and you should put in your claim between the beginning of the fourteenth week and not later than the eleventh week before the baby is due. You are not entitled to the maternity allowance for the weeks in which you are doing paid work. *Beware* – the maternity allowance is payable from 11 weeks before the baby is born and for seven weeks after. If the baby is born later than you expected then you get maternity allowance later *but* if you carry on working after the eleventh week you cannot claim during this period and you cannot make up for it by claiming extra weeks at the end of the inflexible 18 week period. So don't get caught out – as I did – by working on into the 18 week period and thinking you can just claim extra weeks at the end. You cannot.

55

Earnings-related Supplement

This is calculated on your reckonable earnings during the tax year before the one in which you are claiming benefit. This means the total of your earnings as indicated by the amount you paid in National Insurance contributions during the relevant tax year and then divided by 50. There is a current top limit of £120 per week, beyond which payments cease to be earnings-related. You are not entitled to claim earnings-related supplement if you are a married woman who has opted out of paying full National Insurance contribution, or if you are self-employed. While you are receiving maternity allowance you are normally credited with National Insurance contributions, except for the six weeks during which you claim maternity pay. The leaflet which tells you about the earnings-related supplement is NI155A.

Maternity Pay

You are entitled to six weeks' maternity pay if:

1. You have been working for the same employer for at least two years at the beginning of the eleventh week before the week in which the baby is due.

2. You have carried on working up until the beginning of the eleventh week before the week in which the baby is due.

3. You have notified your employer three weeks before you stop work or as soon as is reasonably practical that you will be stopping work because of pregnancy or confinement.

4. You have produced a signed certificate from your doctor or midwife if your employer asks for one.

Maternity pay comes from your employer and represents 90% of a basic week's pay. In other words it takes no account of extras like tips or overtime. The flat rate maternity allowance will be deducted from your maternity pay whether you are entitled to claim it or not. If you are entitled to an *earnings-related* maternity allowance then the idea is that you end up with the equivalent of a full week's wages. Maternity pay is normally paid weekly or monthly, or you can ask for it to be paid as a lump sum. It is taxable. Maternity pay is not conditional on your promising to come back to work.

7   Looking After the Under-fives

The question of working mothers generates most heat and emotion when it comes to considering the mothers of babies or very small children. Latch key children are a hot issue too, but abandoned infants top them by several degrees. This chapter looks at all the different ways in which mothers provide substitute care for little children. If they earn a great deal of money they can afford to pay someone qualified to look after their children in their own home. If they suffer real hardship then they will look for help from an unregistered childminder or from a local council nursery. Unless their hardship is of the multiple kind – a one parent family with other problems – they are very unlikely to find a place in a council nursery. The childminder is the most used – if not the most popular – solution. I shall look at all these ways of caring for small children in turn, but first let us look at the emotional problem of leaving babies and small children.

The enormous problem of arranging satisfactory care of little children, coupled with the fact that the majority of mothers do prefer to keep their babies close to them in the very early years, means that less than one quarter of under-fives have mothers who go out to work. Yudkin and Holme pointed out that '*some mothers for whom the need to work is felt as an urgent necessity may take on a succession of temporary jobs, each one being given up as the arrangements for the care of the children become unsuccessful. Once the women had been at work for six months or more, the chances were that they would stay for a long time.*'

A great many mothers are forced to give up work when their babies are born because they cannot find anyone at all to help them. A qualified occupational therapist – a skill much in demand – reported giving up her job in a teaching hospital psychiatric unit because she could find nobody to help look after her children and she points out that very few hospitals (or any other work places) provide crèches for the children of staff. Many women give the whole thing up as a bad job, like this *Woman's Own* reader.

'*My two children are 5½ and 18 months. I have discovered that there are no nurseries. There are only two childminders near me and they only take one child at a time, or there is the old hit and miss business of advertising for someone and hoping to get someone competent and kind. I cannot feel justified in doing so when I do not absolutely have to. I shall stay at home with my little son. Unfortunately by the time he is old enough to leave I shall be too old to do the training I would have liked to have done.*'

Other mothers cling to their jobs with the help of a rotting patchwork of makeshift arrangements. One mother may shuttle her child from play school to one of three different neighbours. Another may have to juggle one child with a minder and another at a nursery, '*Which doesn't start until 9.30, finishes at 12 midday, so it's useless to me and I've had him staying with someone different practically every day. Why should it be so difficult?*' No wonder that mothers who have to resort in panic to a series of alternative arrangements begin to feel very guilty at the way they seem to be desperately farming out their children. A divorced mother remembers the early years alone with her three children as a nightmare of compromise and guilt, even though she had no choice but to work.

'*I set up a series of diabolical arrangements. I paid for friends to look after them and if that failed then I dragged the children to college with me. One day I remember my two and a half year old clinging to a lamp-post and saying "please don't leave me today, mummy." And the neighbour I'd been leaving him with admitted that she'd lost her temper with him and pulled his hair. If I felt they were upset then I'd take the day off rather than leave them, or take them with me. It was a terrible time. When I was washing up in the guest house next door I could put them to bed and I'd let out a spare room to a lodger who could listen out for them. If I was teaching students English I could take them with me. It was always a mixture. I'd pay a friend – you find you out-live your friends very quickly. I couldn't even afford a childminder – I payed for the service in kind.*'

All this uncertainty about child care has a profound effect on the stage at which mothers feel free to work. One *Woman's Own* reader said that her pregnancy was ruined through worry over finding someone to care for her baby if she went back to work. She was lucky enough to find a good and reliable minder but she was afraid to have another child in case she was not so lucky a second time. '*There is no point,*' she wrote bleakly, '*in job protection for women who are pregnant when there are no facilities to look after their infants.*'

Most women would like to have a decent interval in which to recover from the strain of pregnancy and child-birth and in which to get to know their new baby. If they are determined, for whatever reason, to return to work while their child is still a baby then sooner may be better than later. How soon depends a great deal on the baby himself. Many first-time mothers are surprised to discover that babies are people, that they do not sleep all the time or stick to a set routine. Some babies are settled and contented at six weeks. Others are unpredictable even at six months. Some mothers are seduced by their babies into abandoning thoughts of work altogether. They did not realise that the babies would be so absorbing or interesting. Others are rather alarmed by the strength of the bond they feel forming and actually need to distance themselves from their baby in order to be in control.

Assuming that you do want to return to work and that your baby is an 'average' baby who has happily settled into his own routine by about three months, to the extent that you feel you can safely leave him in somebody else's loving and competent care, then many experts recommend that you start sooner rather than later. A little baby is not yet so aware of his surroundings and the people who form part of them that he will be as distressed when you take to disappearing for regular periods as an older child might be. Once he is a little older, say eight or nine months, then he will definitely be more closely attached to you and more likely to be upset by sudden separation. There is a case for saying that if you cannot begin to leave your baby early you should wait until he is old enough to understand more clearly what is going on.

Whenever you decide to return to work and leave your child in someone else's care, the more time you can spend in settling your child gradually, the happier you both will be. It is thoughtless and cruel to take a small child along to a strange place, whether a childminder's house or a crèche, and leave him suddenly with people he does not know and with no certainty that you will return. He is bound to be very unhappy. Introduce him to his new caretaker bit by bit. If you have someone coming to your home, be there while he gets used to them, for several days if need be. Try leaving him for short periods. Gradually he will grow used to the idea that you always come back when you go out. If you take him to a childminder or a nursery, visit it with him for short periods beforehand. Talk to him about it. Stay with him until he seems to be happy with the staff or the other children. The first time you leave him, tell him what you are doing and tell him that you will come back. Go as you said you would, and come back, as you said you would.

Whatever you do, your attitude will communicate itself to your child. If you feel terribly guilty and apologetic he will sense that the situation is upsetting and that you will be receptive to any fuss he makes. Nursery staff told me about one little girl who took more than six months to settle happily into a work-place crèche – normally it should take no more than two weeks. The problem was the mother's obvious, glaring guilt at leaving her child and her own lack of conviction about working in the first place. Each morning she would deliver the child to the nursery and enact a drama. *'Never mind, darling,'* she would say tearfully, *'Mother will be back soon. Don't worry. I know you miss me. Mummy misses you too. Don't be upset.'* This exhausting exchange of guilt, tears and kisses left the child upset for the rest of the morning. If you are matter-of-fact, confident and, above all, consistent, about what you are doing then your child will take his cue from your behaviour.

You may be worried about whether your child will be harmed by his separation from you at such an early stage. If your child is normally resilient and if you handle the separation sensitively then it will not only not harm a child, it can do him good. Probably more good than it will do you to start with. A mother who, through force of circumstance, took her 14 month old to a nursery spent every morning for six weeks in a flood of tears until the matron of the nursery took her in hand and told her not to be so wet. *'She loves it here,'* she said. *'She adores playing with the other children and she's getting lots of benefit out of it.'*

Small children are capable of enjoying the company of other children at a much earlier age than is often supposed. The Pre-school Playgroups Association, for example, will not have children under three in its playgroups. Three is the statutory age for nursery education to start and it is supposed to be the age at which children begin to benefit properly from mixing with other children. But tiny children of 18 months and less can get a great deal from each other's company, and regular periods safely playing in the company of others of the same age can give a child a great deal of stimulation and confidence. Your child may well be playing with toys, in spaces, with people that you cannot supply him with at home. Flat-bound city children, in particular, get a lot out of going to a bright, lively place where they can run around, play with messy paints and sand and water, climb frames, ride tricycles and learn how other children behave.

The main danger to small children comes from insecurity. There is a case for saying that even if the arrangement you make is imperfect – as long as it is not harmful – you should stick to it and make up the gaps at home. Perfect care for small children does not exist. *You* are not perfect. You get crabby or inattentive or bored, however brilliant a mother you might try to be and your child gets crabby and bored with you from time to time and no nursery or minder is going to be perfect either. There will always be some aspect of your child's care that will niggle you, but *as long as the child seems happy*, remind yourself that consistency of care is as important as quality. The child who suffers most, according to many studies, is the child who is subject to a series of different care arangements even when these may be a swift series of marvellous, highly trained nannies. Learning to get along with other imperfect human beings as well as yourself is one of the most valuable lessons your child can learn. But he needs time to learn it. Don't bewilder him by moving him from one person's care just as he is getting used to their peculiarities and beginning to trust himself to them. And don't undermine your child's affection for these new people in his life. His feelings for his childminder or his nanny or nursery nurse are no threat to his feelings for you. The more people a human being learns to love in security, the better and the more confidently he will grow.

These are the basic principles of entrusting your child to a stranger's care. Here are the facts about finding and arranging that care. At the last count there were 30,333 registered childminders providing places for 91,878 children. There were 27,000 places in local authority day nurseries. There were 2,400 places in work-place nurseries and crèches and there were 22,000 places in private day nurseries. That makes 143,278 places in registered day care for small children of working mothers. But 850,000 children under five have mothers who work part- or full-time. That leaves 706,722 children who are looked after in some other unrecorded way – presumably a patchwork of friends, relations, unregistered minders and neighbours – a staggering indication of the hopeless inadequacy of proper day care for under-fives in this country. What it means is that if you have children under five and you want to go out to work, even part-time, your chances of finding properly organised care for your children are negligible.

You will notice that I have not mentioned two major areas of – let us call it occupation, not care – for under-fives. One of these is the playgroup movement; the other is nursery education. The reason that I do not go into either of these in this book is that this is a book for working mothers looking for day care for their children and neither playgroups nor nursery schools provide a day care service. They provide stimulation, company, entertainment, education – all kinds of good things – but they are not designed to look after children during the working day. In certain areas there are extended nursery classes which add on child care at the end of a normal school day and I will look at these later on.

In their survey on facilities for working mothers and their children, *Woman's Own* found more than half the mothers they questioned wanted properly run day nurseries for their children. Only two per cent wanted more childminders, but childminders are the most common solution to the day care problem.

CHILDMINDERS

A childminder is anyone who is not a relative who looks after your child for you in the minder's own home, for more than two hours a day, for pay. A childminder is legally obliged to be registered with the local Social Services Department, and if she is unregistered she is liable to pay a £50 fine or serve three months in jail. Mothers are constantly advised not to leave their children with an unregistered childminder, as though unregistered minders are necessarily Dickensian in their awfulness, and registered childminders' care guaranteed to be an officially approved mother substitute. The truth of the matter is that there may be as many as ten unregistered minders to one registered minder and that registration is absolutely no guarantee of quality. The official figures say that 91,878 children are placed with minders. The last unofficial estimate suggests that it is nearer 330,000 if you include unregistered minders. Mothers who are desperate to keep a job leave their children with almost anyone, and certainly do not stop to check some official registration. If, for 'childminder' you read 'an ordinary lady who lives down the street,' nothing seems more obvious and natural than to leave your child in her neighbourly care, in a private home and to come to some informal arrangement about payment. It is fashionable to say that a good minder is the best of all arrangements for looking after small children but good minders are hard to find and bad minders – of which there are many – can cause irreparable harm to your children. The very informality of the arrangement means that it is full of pitfalls.

'Childminders,' wrote one Woman's Own reader, 'are unsatisfactory because one doesn't know how much to pay the minder and because one can be let down so much. One minder left without so much as a day's notice because I was half an hour late from school and was unable to let her know. It would help everyone if childminding was regarded as a proper job with standard rates of pay and notice procedure.'

'Although I was able to find a girl minder near my work,' wrote another, 'so that I could feed my baby at lunch time and later, play with him, I still suffered from guilt feelings and lack of identification later. And I'm sure he cried a lot at night because he was deprived of my company, or any one else's for that matter. And at weekends, and once I had left at the end of the school year he was a different child. Whilst some babyminders are excellent, the whole relationship between mother and minder tends to be too personal and amateur. The mother often feels guilty and the minder exploited and the mother has to seek out the minder on her own behalf.'

Seeking out the minder in the first place can be a harrowing experience. If a minder is registered, then the local Social Services Department will be able to give you her name and address, but because there are relatively few registered minders, if a minder is any good she will be turning mothers away. The registration procedure is entirely aimed at checking certain physical facilities and screening out only the absolutely criminal. 'The law,' say Brian and Sonia Jackson in their revelatory book, Childminder, 'is entirely negative, largely time consuming, most intrusive, implicitely insulting and utterly unrealistic. I am astonished that we have any childminders at all.'

If a woman wishes to become a childminder she must make a declaration of good health, have an X-ray, sign a statement saying that she has never been convicted of an offence against a child or young person or had a child taken into care or had a nervous or similar illness. An inspector from the Social Services Department will visit the minder's home and check that it has sufficient space, that its fires are guarded, its steps gated off, that it is a safe place for children to be. The requirements of the law are much more stringent than is normal in every day life. A childminder showed me a list of regulations that said that no child was ever to be allowed into the kitchen without adult supervision. How many mothers could say that their children never go into the kitchen on their own? None I would imagine.

Having checked the minder's home, the Social Services Department then recommend that she should be registered to look after a certain number of children – usually no more than three and sometimes only one. The registration process can take as long as 18 months, which is absolutely discouraging to the minder and any mother who is hoping to use her services. This is probably the main reason why there are so few registered minders. In one London borough, three out of four prospective minders withdrew before the process was over, and one can only assume that they went into business on their own account without bothering to register. Unregistered minders are on a fairly safe wicket because there are never more than five prosecutions a year.

You will note that nowhere in this registration process is any kind of check made into what the child will *do* when it is with the minder. No help has to be offered in the way of training or back-up facilities. Because officials are checking for externals like clean lavatories, they do not notice whether the place is actually welcoming to children. I visited a childminder once who lived in an immaculate house, but every child height surface was covered with little glass animals. When my curious two year old reached for them she was instantly stopped. There was nothing in the minder's house to indicate that a child could play happily and safely. It was an *adult* house.

If a mother draws a blank at the local Social Services Department she is driven underground in her search for a minder. The demand for minders is greatest in working-class areas in big cities, and it is especially high among immigrant (largely West Indian) communities, who consequently suffer from the worst of the childminding system.

You only have to look in newsagents' windows in residential urban areas to find the little cards advertising a minder's services. Or, as one young West Indian mother once told me, '*if you see someone down the main street with kids, you stop and ask them if they know a minder in the area.*' The National Childminding Study conducted what they called 'Dawnwatch' and once, as a reporter, I did it myself. It means going to a working-class district very early in the morning and watching the parents of young children rushing them along the streets on their way to work and handing them over at certain doors. That is where the minders live. If the children are unlucky they may never come out of that door – or even out of one room behind it – until their parents collect them again in the evening.

If the children are lucky and their mother has found a good minder, then they will be as happy, secure and well cared for as they might be in their own home. Mothers of small babies in particular may be keen to find a good minder, because the mother knows that she can provide the gentle home comforts and the attention that small babies need. A good minder is somebody you can trust to treat your child as you would yourself. Preferably she will have had some training or will have children of her own. She might be a nurse or teacher who has given up work to look after her own children and has decided to look after one or two more. You will be able to tell a lot about her as soon as you go into her house. Is it pristine and untouchable or are there plenty of toys for the children to play with? If there are toys, are they well-chosen toys to suit children of different ages and are they out within the children's reach, not put away on a high shelf? (Bad minders do not have toys because they think that toys are too much trouble and make the children squabble.) Is there a safe, pleasant outdoor area for the children to play in or do they have to spend the whole day in one room? Does she take the children out every day? Taking them shopping is better than nothing, but a really good minder will try to take the children to a park or to a playgroup.

Ask the minder how she organises her day. Does she have a system in which the children have a mixture of activity, set times for milk and biscuits and rest? What does she give them for lunch and tea? Are you expected to provide the food or does she cook them a meal each day? Watch the way she behaves with the children. Does she constantly stop them doing things? Is she patient and attentive? If a child seems genuinely upset, does she pick him up and cuddle him? Ask her how she will cope if your child is unhappy when you leave. Do not be afraid – however anxious you are to find someone to take care of your children – to

65

grit your teeth and persist in looking for someone better if a child-minder does seem unsuitable.

'*Social Services offered me the choice of one childminder,*' reported one *Woman's Own* reader. '*I was most unhappy as she lived on the eleventh floor of a tower block, did not go out very much and seemed to leave the children much to themselves. I managed to find a very good childminder who is not only an intelligent person but also takes the children to the local nursery school for the morning so I think I've got the best of both worlds with a loving mother figure to provide the personal attention, care and cuddles that small children require, and also the stimulating environment of the pre-school nursery.*'

Note that the first childminder – on the eleventh floor of a tower block and uninterested in children – was registered on the council's list. Even if you find what seems to be a good childminder, do not, in your relief at having found a solution, relax your guard. You must check constantly that your child is receiving good care and if you cannot check, see if a neighbour or friend can keep an eye open for you. You might have the experience of this mother who found somebody who seemed eminently suitable but proved to be a disaster.

'*I found an ex-nurse with two small children who seemed very suitable. All went well for a short time until my eldest daughter became very withdrawn over a half-term holiday. They were never taken out except to friends' houses and it was a very hot summer. I later found, on arriving early one evening that a bedroom (very small) had been shut off and the children stayed in there for most of the day with the eldest daughter of the minder.*'

This indifference represents one of the worst hazards of childminding. Too many women who undertake childminding do it as a way of earning what they see as easy money without stirring from their own homes. They are not interested in children, they know little about them and they certainly do not see the need to educate or stimulate them in any way. At worst there are proven horror stories about rows of babies left unchanged in cots and garages with bottles propped up against their faces and their feed running into sore ears. But neglect of mind is as harmful as physical neglect. The children most affected by the worst of childminding are West Indian. Between one half and two thirds of young West Indian mothers work and have their children minded, and the children can spend day after day just sitting in one room, unspoken to, unplayed with. While they are at the minder's they are silent and apathetic but once they reach school they face real difficulties in adapting. Either they go completely wild in the open spaces and stimulating environment or they stay silent and apathetic and unreceptive.

It is ironical that the 'easy' money made by childminding is actually very little from the minder's point of view. She works very long hours – in the worst-off areas factory working mothers can leave their children at 6.30 or 7.00 in the morning and not pick them up again until 12 hours later. This can mean a child being woken as early as 5.30 in order to make the journey to the minder, and not returning home until 8.00 at night. The payment that a mother must make a minder for a full working week averages £15. It can be much lower than that if the minder is unregistered and makes up in numbers what she lacks in individual fees. It can be higher than that for a good minder in somewhere like central London. It is a noticeable lump out of a mother's salary, but it is hardly an excessive wage for the minder. It works out at about 30p per hour.

An average childminder works a ten hour day and very few of them charge overtime if the mother is late. They expect and are entitled to bank holidays and holidays themselves. They often find themselves forking out for unconsidered extras. A study carried out by the National Childminding Association found that one third of minders paid the child's playgroup fees, for example.

The existence of the National Childminding Association is an encouraging sign that this isolated but enormous group of women wish to be better organised and to improve the image of the childminder. Childminders usually share the problems of the women whose children they care for. They work long hours, are confined to the home, are badly paid, untrained and with no hope of change or promotion. Increasing efforts are being made, depending a great deal on the quality of the local Social Services Department, to break this circle of isolation and ignorance. Minders are encouraged to meet regularly, to bring their children into a nursery regularly, to join toy libraries and to attend special lectures. This is cheering news for the pressure groups who would like to see the central place of childminding in the child care system acknowledged and supported. The most radical approach to improving childminding lies in childminding services being organised by the local authority, or by an interested employer. This would take away the childminder's freelance status in many cases, and make her a salaried employee. It would mean that childminders were trained and that certain standards of care and education were maintained and supervised and – most welcome of all to mothers – that a proper registration system could be organised so that mother and minder could be matched and a waiting list organised. In an ideal world childminders would be organised from a children's centre where they could use a toy and book library and bring their charges to a playgroup. Until that day comes, it is up to mother and minder to battle the thing out together. Better mothers make better minders.

DAY NURSERIES

Most studies into what care mothers want for their children, both in Britain and abroad, prove tht nurseries are the most popular answer. Childminding is too personal, uncontrollable, unreliable. A properly run day nursery with professionally trained staff can have faults too, but it guarantees a basic standard of care, it provides good physical facilities, and it is reliable. The trouble is that it is also non-existent as far as most working mothers are concerned. Nurseries of all kinds – private nurseries, factory crèches and council nurseries – provide only 51,000 places. Your chances of getting a child into a council or local authority nursery are very slender indeed. Unless you are a single mother there is really little point in trying, and even if you are a single mother you had better not look too competent. Council nurseries seem to be taken up by the children of problem families referred by a social worker. They are not a practical solution for the ordinary working mother, even for divorcees like this *Woman's Own* reader.

'*I'm a divorced single parent. When my daughter first started nursery at fifteen months old there was a long waiting list. The nursery catered for sixty children from six weeks old up to school age. The charge was £1.25 a day for working mums and 62½p for non-working. To get a child in you had to be single or on the verge of a nervous break down or both, and had to seek the help of a social worker before a child would be admitted.*'

'*As for nurseries,*' said another, '*I couldn't even get on a waiting list so there can be no statistics to show how many people requiring day care for their children are unsatisfied. It's my impression that you can only get your child into a council nursery if your husband won't work and if you are mentally disturbed.'*

A certain vicious circle can set itself up when mothers get a place in a local authority day nursery. Because the places are so limited the mother is under pressure to keep working and to keep that place whatever the cost. The mothers who use them are the mothers in most need and so they work long hours. The nursery is rarely in the next street, so this means a tiring journey at either end of the day and a child who hardly sees his parents or his mother during the working week. The physical care of babies and small children is so demanding that the staff can often spend more time in cleaning up and changing nappies than they do in play and talk, and older, nursery school age children who attend them because of their mothers' working hours, have their educational needs neglected altogether.

If you are very lucky you may have a crèche or day nursery (the terms are interchangeable) at your work-place, but these only provide 2,400 places in all. The best of them are very good and they have the advantage of being geographically close to the mother so that she does not have a double journey and she is to hand if she wishes to see her child during the day or if her child needs her. Women are constantly campaigning for work-place crèches; if there were as many crèches as there are campaigns then the problem would be half solved, but many experts are suspicious of them. They look on work-place crèches as the equivalent of the farm labourer's tied cottage, a seeming benefit that only ties the labourer to his employer and allows him to be exploited in other ways. I disagreed with this argument until I read the following letter from a *Woman's Own* reader.

'I started work at an electrical component factory for the simple reason that (a) I needed the money and (b) they had a nursery that they ran themselves. The only snag was that the wages were very low, starting at 55p an hour which, after I had been there ten months, were put up to 70p an hour although I was working from nine until five, five days a week. Altogether I worked for 33 hours for £23. After that I had to pay for the nursery which amounted to £2.50 a week which I regard as reasonable. But I soon started paying tax and the nursery fees were put up to £5 a week. Because of this my wages became so whittled down that I handed in my notice.'

Costs of work-place nurseries are often subsidised by

employers, but even this can be a threat to their existence if the employer suddenly decides, because of a recession, or a drop in the female labour force, that the expense is not justified. Women who need nurseries are prepared to pay more for them than idealistic planners suppose. One mother was outraged to find that the nursery at her work-place was closed down just as she took her maternity leave and planned to return to work. *'I knew that at the time it was set up it had been over-subscribed by at least three children for every place. I was told that it had been closed because it was a drain on funds because they made no charge. As you can imagine I was astounded and disgusted to think of all those frustrated mothers and children who were turned away and who could have been so easily catered for for want of a little effort and consideration.'*

Failing a work-place crèche you may consider a private nursery. Private day nurseries provide only 22,000 places and the cost here is much higher than a pound a day, nor can there be any subsidised fee for low-earning mothers; £20 a week is not at all uncommon. In fact the sheer expense of setting up and staffing a day nursery is probably the major reason for their absence. I do not have to tell mothers how very demanding small children are, or how much work and attention they represent. Staff ratios differ from council to council, but one member of staff to anywhere between six and eight children is normal.

When it comes to small babies their ratio shoots up to one to three. That makes babies very expensive, but it is also an indication of the kind of care a baby can expect in even the best run nursery. One small baby is a full-time job for most mothers. It does not take much thought to see that if one person is expected to care simultaneously for three small babies, then the chances of at least one of those babies being left unattended and perhaps crying at any one time are very high. I have to declare a personal belief that nurseries are not the best place for little babies. However, as most nurseries do not have the staff or the facilities, such as a milk kitchen, necessary to care for babies, this is rather an academic problem.

Private nurseries have the advantage that the children are likely to be less demanding of the staff's time than the many disturbed children in some council nurseries. This means that staff can spend more time in play activity than in coping with emotional crises. The whole question of staff ratios is irrational in any case. As one nursery administrator pointed out to me, '*they say you have to have a one to five staff ratio in a nursery, but if it's a nursery school then you might only have to have one member of staff and a helper to twenty children. The fact is, it's a child you're looking after and they're all under five and you need that ratio whatever you're doing with them.*'

Places are as scarce in private nurseries as they are in local authority nurseries but do not be afraid to try your luck, even if it looks as though the nursery is confined to a special group of people – a university crèche for example. Often a nursery which has taken all the children of the employees or students entitled to use it will hve a place or two left over and will be only too happy to take the children of outsiders. Their overhead costs are the same, after all, and they all need the fees.

The quality of a day nursery depends, more than any other factor, on the quality of the staff who run it. If you are fortunate enough to have a choice of nurseries to look at before you decide where to place your child, do not be entirely seduced by lots of bright, new equipment, spacious, light rooms and good play space. People are what count. This description of a modern show-place nursery in France is a beady-eyed summing up of one of the problems.

'*In Rheims we visited show place crèches built or adapted to the highest standards and lavishly equipped. All the walls and furniture had rounded edges to prevent bumps and bruises, everything was clean, bright and airy with great attention to hygiene and health care. But in some ways the scene was all too familiar. There were children, mostly sitting very quietly in their plastic moulded chairs, surrounded by gaily coloured toys, the spotless walls decorated with Walt Disney cut outs, overlooked by a handful of bored looking girls talking to each other about their boyfriends. Clearly they didn't see their role as educational.*'

The crux of the problem with day care for children under five is that it falls between two governmental stools, the Department of Health and Social Services and the Department of Education. The Social Services side of the coin sees the job as one of childminding, physical care and prevention from harm. The Education Department is much more positive in its approach to small children. Trained nursery teachers know what can be done to encourage curiosity and skills and to give little children all the opportunities they need to flourish mentally and socially. But trained nursery teachers do not get near the majority of children of working mothers because the nursery schools where they work are not open at hours which match the mother's work.

The staff of day nurseries are almost entirely qualified nursery nurses with unqualified assistants, but the qualification they have, the NNEB or National Nursery Education Board, is not necessarily a guarantee of sympathy and understanding for children. Carole Cowan, the Director of a company called Kindergartens for Commerce, which advises on and supplies crèches to work-places, described the difficulty of finding the ideal staff for a nursery.

'In Sweden or Denmark, girls who want to work with children have to do a year or two years as a nanny or mother's help before they start their training. But every September I get girls starting with me straight from their training who drop out after a week or two because they didn't "realise it was like this", by which they mean changing nappies and things. There are a lot of girls with the NNEB who are not particularly talented with children. I've got a girl now who's hopeless. She has no creative ability at all. She has to be told absolutely everything. They lack the ability to originate. They give them all these studies and psychology but they've never had to run a nursery. What I look for is if a girl likes children and is patient – that's very important – and has a nice way with children. There are many girls who would make marvellous nursery nurses but who aren't academically brilliant and don't get the qualifications. You have to mother the children. You're a mother substitute and you've got to be able to kiss and cuddle them.'

Mrs Cowan also feels very strongly about the Social Services oar in the nursery pond. 'The Social Services only call once every three months and they know nothing. They're interested in lavatories and wash hand basins but they don't pay any attention to what we're doing to these children's minds while they're with us.'

If you care about what happens to your child's mind all day while you are out at work, then your gut reaction to the nursery atmosphere is very important. Are children left crying or wandering aimlessly about? Do the staff seem alert to what the children are doing or do they seem to prefer chatting among themselves or to any visitors who come into the nursery? Do the staff seem competent? Do they seem loving? What kinds of activities do the children do during the day and are they well balanced to provide a natural rhythm of active and quiet play? Is there a quiet place where little children can rest or a certain time of the day when all the children are put down to sleep? If so, how long do they stay resting?

Is there plenty of messy, explorative play like water bowls and sand trays and paint? Ask the staff what they do if children are difficult and naughty. Do you see them smack a child, and if you do, do you mind? Or do they have a firm policy of not touching the children? Do the children have their own work on display on the walls as evidence that they do organise creative work and are encouraged to be proud of it? Or are all the pretty murals done by the staff? And, very important, what is the staff's attitude to parents? Do they encourage you to stay with your child and break him in gently or do you get the impresion that parents should hand their children over swiftly at the door and then leave them to it?

In order to find your nursery, your first port of call should be your local Social Services Department. They will be able to tell you of any local authority nurseries in your area and, since they have to approve all nursery provision, they can also tell you about the private nurseries. One of the big advantages of day nurseries is supposed to be their reliability and the fact that they are always there, properly staffed and open at hours that suit working mothers, but mothers should be aware that nurseries are very vulnerable to spending cuts of any kind, whether local or national. If you get your child into a good nursery, then you should be prepared to battle from time to time to keep that nursery open. Employers who set up work-places crèches to attract female staff at a time when the economy is rising, suddenly see the project as a white elephant at a time when they are laying employees off. When government spending cuts in public services are imposed upon local authorities, care of any kind for under-fives is among the first areas to be threatened. An old-age pensioner in Manchester told *Woman's Own* about her part in keeping a local nursery open, simply because nobody before her had bothered to raise the matter.

'*Four years ago Trafford council decided to close the local day nursery. One evening I attended a meeting and asked a Councillor why they were closing the nursery. He said nobody had complained. I went home and asked a niece whose daughter went to the nursery to write a letter stating why she wished the nursery to remain open. The following morning she spoke to all the mothers there asking them to write. I asked the local shop keeper if she had heard any complaints. She had. I left her the address to write to. Also an outline of the complaint. In addition I wrote to the Councillor giving my opinion of the damage the closure would do to the mothers and children, many of whom lived in high-rise flats. Three days later I received a letter saying they were considering the closure. The nursery is still open. This proves that local people should be aware of any moves that affect them and act accordingly.'*

Nobody is happy about the scattered, disorganised, vulnerable supply of official day care for little children. What there is may not be the best care for children and it is certainly a continuing worry and strain on their mothers. It is an area which is under constant review by various interested bodies (though not by many politicians who mostly give the impression that they would like it to go away). Future solutions to the problems of institutional day care are evolving along lines which aim to keep the best of the childminding and the best group care and which would involve an attempt to meet all of a child's needs – for physical care and protection and for education – in the one centre. The Trades Union Congress, for example, believes in places called 'nursery centres' which would unite the day care and the educational element and provide a focus for childminding services in the area. The day nursery would employ teachers, and the nursery classes for older children would provide extended day care to help the children of working mothers. Childminders, they believe, should be employed directly by the local authority and should be attached to a local nursery centre where they could find professional support and playgroups for their children.

One such centre already in existence is the Thomas Coram Centre in London's Bloomsbury which provides a real children's haven for the surrounding communities. It is set in a green and spacious complex of squares and playgrounds and it houses a nursery and a welfare clinic, toy and book libraries, and a mother and toddler group. It manages the hitherto impossible feat of employing nursery nurses and teachers on the same scheme and it is jointly financed by Social Services and by Education. Teachers and nurses work in one staffing hierarchy, and work shifts and staggered hours to cover the activities of the Centre. Some children only come to the Centre for a couple of hours, some come all day, every day, and it is open to anybody who lives within a half mile radius.

Far more three to five year old children could be helped by the extension of nursery school hours to match the adult working day. One London borough, Islington, already does this by providing play activities after normal school hours. But nursery schools are subject to the same threatened cuts and instabilities as local authority nurseries. Nevertheless, like after-care and holiday schemes for older children, this is a sensible and cost effective use of school facilities and offers a real service to working mothers. It also has the advantage of giving the children stimulating, educational care rather than the routine childminding service of a bad day nursery.

In certain cases parents have got together to establish community nurseries staffed by paid professional workers, usually based in an ordinary adapted house or old building and run by parent committees with plenty of voluntary help. If the idea of setting up your own day care centre in this way interests you, you can find out more about how to do it in Chapter Nine.

HOME HELP

The rich, as always, know a good thing when they see it. There are enormous advantages to having a sort of Mary Poppins on tap at home. If you are grand enough to afford a special nursery floor (which I am assured the best nannies require before they will set foot in your house) and a colour television for your nanny, then you are free from child care 24 hours a day – if that is what you want. It is curious that the mothers who do go for this kind of arrangement are not usually working mothers but mothers who have all this and leisure too.

What a working mother needs is somebody less grand, somebody who is not above doing the shopping, or running the Hoover round the sitting room, or washing up the breakfast because everyone else was in too much of a rush to get it done. The fact that this someone is there, in her own house, means that her children are in familiar surroundings, that they can be taken care of at home when they are ill, that the mother can come and go in absolute confidence that all is well. No rushing to take or collect the child from the nursery. No worrying what the child might be getting to eat at the childminder's. No panic if the mother is held up at work. When your children are looked after in their own home you have much more control over every aspect of the situation.

Of course this convenience does not come cheap, which is why home help is something for the very few. Jane Reid, head of The Nanny Service, told me that an experienced mother's help of 17 to 18 earns around £20 per week living-in. As she gets more experienced it goes up to £25 or £30. If she lives out, then she will expect to get at least £40, plus her National Insurance stamp. The well-trained but inexperienced nanny expects £35 a week after tax living-in, and an experienced nanny, living-in, expects to earn between £40 and £50 after tax – this represents £70 a week to the mother. On top of that there is the original fee to the agency of around 2½ weeks net wages.

You can see from this that it is expensive all round, and that it is much cheaper if you have the space to have somebody living-in. If you do have the space in your house to have somebody living-in then it is cheaper still to have an au pair girl, but these bring other problems in their train. They are not meant to be treated as full-time domestic help and if you have very small children in the house, you may not want them cared for by somebody who can hardly speak English. Au pair girls may, or may not, be interested in children or have experience with them and if you do intend to get an au pair girl to help you with your children you would do well to spell this out loud and clear before you accept her.

The best time of year to find an au pair, according to London's Au Pair Bureau, is from July 1st onwards, when the girls are queuing up for summer jobs. So an au pair might be a good solution to fill the school holiday gap, even if you don't want one for the whole year. In order to employ an au pair girl you have to offer her her own bedroom and somewhere between £12 and £15 a week pocket money. Her main purpose in coming to Britain is to learn English, so she is only expected to work about five hours a day and she must have regular time off to attend classes. In return, she will help you with light house work and she is expected to be available for at least two evenings' baby-sitting a week.

A further disadvantage of the au pair, from the point of view of the mother of young children who form close attachments, is that the average stay is dropping from a year to six months. This has been hastened by a recent Home Office ruling that only Western European girls between the ages of seventeen and twenty seven can qualify as au pairs – thus ruling out all those Japanese, Philippinos and Israelis who, coming from further afield, could be guaranteed to stay longer.

Another cut-price solution is to take on a probationary nanny from the Norland Nursery Training College which trains nannies for the nobility and the Arabs. Each trained girl has to do a nine months' probationary period in a private house before she is fully qualified and if you take her during this stage you will only have to pay her £40 a week plus board and lodging. You also have to give her £20 uniform allowance and provide her with her own room plus a day and night nursery which rules most of us out again. Only the rich can afford cheap nannies.

Although they seem like the perfect solution, if you can afford it, nannies of various grades are not without their problems as you find if you decide to advertise for one on the open market. One way to find a nanny or mother's help is to go to a specialised agency (see the addresses at the end of the book). The other traditional way is to advertise in either *The Lady* or *Nursery World*. Advertisements in *The Lady* often turn out to be shrimping nets on the sea bottom of life. They can either turn up the perfect treasure or what one advertiser described as *'a lot of terrifyingly awful people'*.

'A rum collection,' said one mother reflectively. *'Middle-aged ladies wanting uniforms, people who'd marched out on their husbands and wanted somewhere to live. Young country girls who wanted to live in London and were only recently qualified. I was looking for someone to live in because we have the space and it was cheaper. In the end I heard about Marion through friends. She has been with us six years now. I wanted someone who was solid and reliable, had patience and was fond of children. We were so nervous in the role of employers that we leant over backwards to tell people how nice we'd be to work for.'*

'The stress comes in finding help,' said one mother who commutes fifty miles from her children each day and needs to know that the help she has left at home is absolutely reliable. *'I wanted somebody to run the house and care for the children with the emphasis on care. I saw a stupendous amount of terrifyingly awful people. They seemed to want the reflected glory of working for a career woman. I decided to spell it out, exactly what I wanted because I didn't want them turning round and saying "you never said I was to wash the dishes", or anything. I got forty applications. A lot of them lacked experience and I was determined to have someone who could cope in a crisis. I have my spy systems and I keep an eye on them. My mother looks in from time to time. Then I have a daily cleaner who is very sensible and there are neighbours and other mothers at school. The thing that worried me was that one child was ill and I came home and found that Cynthia hadn't*

put her to bed even though she had a temperature of 102. She said her mother would never have sent her to bed for a thing like that. But once she's got it into her head that I'm over-protective then she'll behave differently next time.'

Another mother who advertised in *The Lady* found that nannying is a sellers' market. '*If they're any good and you don't take them on the spot, that's it. I found a very nice girl to live-in but she got homesick and went back to the country. She didn't know a soul in London and she was sitting at home with the baby all day so she didn't get to know anyone either. I think this is one of the problems of the job. People say "who on earth would like to sit in somebody's home all day and look after babies", but there are girls who love it. This one will set off to take my little girl to the swimming baths and end up taking five kids out of choice – on a journey that means changing buses twice and walking quite a way.'*

Another of the problems with employing a nanny, as opposed to sending your child to a nursery or to a minder is the emotional situation. A child is inevitably going to become very much attached to a nice person who comes to play with him everyday and this can cause problems. If you change your nanny frequently, then your child is no better off than one who is moved from minder to minder. His security is threatened. But if the nanny stays long enough for a deep attachment to grow, then when she inevitably goes, it can be like losing a second mother figure. How you treat this situation depends on how deliberately you keep your place in your child's life. It is possible for your children to realise quite clearly who is in charge, especially if the nanny is somebody who comes in during the day and you are the person who is always there the rest of the time.

'*I had a fantastic nanny,*' reports one mother. '*She was competent and good and nice and she stayed with us for five years. I listened to her talking to my little girl sometimes and I'd think "she's being a bit harsh", but I felt I'd handed over responsibility to her each day and I shouldn't conflict with her. There was never any confusion with the nanny because I was always there. I was always in charge and in evenings and at weekends I did everything. She never called for the nanny in the night.'*

Where the emotional relationship between child and nanny grows very strong there can be real heart-break. A mother reports trauma when her child's nanny left, even though the mother herself was a very maternal person who worked at home a great deal of the time. The nanny came while the child was still a baby and she was what the mother calls 'a phenomenon'. '*I advertised in*

The Lady for a daily nanny and I found a remarkable person who stayed with us for four years. My daughter developed as having two mothers. The day she left us I had a severe emotional crisis and so did my daughter. She ran a temperature for ten days – the guilt was just awful. Di told her she was going about a week before but the girl picked up that the situation was emotionally charged and the atmosphere was all very tense. She screamed at night and I think she thought I was going too. The GP says he sees this behaviour in divorces when one parent goes. We couldn't make up our minds at first whether Di should come and visit or not. Now she's really part of the family. Help is the crucial factor. At the moment I've got a competent, moody, difficult eighteen year old and it's like having another child in the house.'

It is not only the child who can find the close relationship with a nanny difficult. Modern mothers, with no experience of employing another person in the house, can get in a great muddle when it comes to striking the right note with someone they pay to work for them. The most common mistake is to bend over backwards to be nice and friendly. Jane Reid of the Nanny Service advises a more professional approach.

'You should always take references. Girls can take advantage if you're too soft and once you've allowed them too much rope then you can't reel them back in again. You should start as you mean to go on. Over-familiarity with the nanny is a problem. If one minute you're really good friends and the next minute you have to tell her off about something, it's difficult. A good nanny will keep a distance. A really professional nanny who is clever and sensitive will not allow the children to get too close, but it's often the mother's fault. If the mother comes in each evening and she can't be bothered to go upstairs and say goodnight to the children, if it's always the nanny who tucks them in and kisses them good night, then the children are going to attach themselves to the person who's bringing them up.'

Whether you advertise for a nanny or go through an employment agency, the moment comes when you have to interview her, and decide whether she is the person that you want to look after your child.

The essence of the relationship between employer and employee, as in marriage, is give and take. The biggest failing of the nice middle-class working mother who is likely to be employing a nanny for the first time is a need to be liked, coupled with guilt at employing a nanny in the first place. This makes her a sitting duck. Decide firmly in advance what you can and can't put up with, because once the relationship has started to go wrong it can be very difficult to correct. If you can't stand smokers, don't say, in a moment of weakness, that you don't mind if she smokes. If it is essential that the girl is punctual, make it clear that her job depends on her reliability. If constant telephone calls from her boyfriend drive you mad, then be firm and forbid them. You may not like yourself in the role of stern employer, but it is quite easy to be firm and friendly too, if you have the self-confidence and if you start off on the right foot.

Personal factors like these are almost more important than paper qualifications, but the best nannies are trained too. If a top-grade, proper nanny is what you're after, as opposed to a mother's help, then you will expect her to have her NNEB certificate which means that she has done a two year course in the care of babies and small children. It means that she has the basic knowledge but it is no guarantee of natural ability with children or even common sense. Jane Reid explains:

'The training involves some time spent in hospitals. They'll have been in a maternity ward, a paediatric ward. They'll do some practical work in nurseries or private homes. They get a lot of theory on play and nursing care. If they train in a day nursery they will have done their exams at a local centre or through the tech. Then a lot depends on the standard of teaching whether they are good or not. There is another certificate, the National Association of Maternal and Child Welfare and this course is more geared to private nursing. It teaches them more about what happens at home, about parents and family life and if they're in a tech. it'll stand them in better stead.'

'But common sense is all important. You can get highly trained nannies who have not proved their worth. They'll be over confident. They'll produce good references but then they'll let a toddler play in the traffic. They won't think about a latch left loose on a door. We had a girl recently who was knowledgeable on paper and she had the qualifications and so on but she couldn't handle the job, which was to look after a toddler and a baby. She couldn't even change a nappy properly and she hadn't thought out that she'd have to feed them at different times.'

When you are interviewing ask your potential nanny what she did before she came to you. Why did she leave her last job? Did she complete her training and if not, why not? Is her health good? Try to avoid sounding so grateful at the idea of anyone helping you out that you will let them have a completely free hand. Sound her out on discipline. Don't just say 'what are your views on punishment?' Ask her what she would do if a child refused to eat or if an older child hit a younger one. Don't ask her if she plays with the children. Ask her what kind of games she thinks are suitable for a year old baby or a three year old toddler. Ask her what kind of food she can cook for the child and make clear from the start any of your own funny little ways about which you feel strongly. If your children never have sweets or do have dummies or always get put to bed at a certain time, let her know. And let her know the worst of it as well. If you expect her to do the family shopping and Hoover the house, then she ought to know about that before she starts.

Personal like plays a great part, of course. If something in you dislikes and distrusts the nanny then trust your instinct. But once you have made up your mind, be business-like. Draw up a written list of conditions of work, including her right to holidays and time off, and make sure that she sees and agrees to it before you finally commit yourself. You will probably be liable to pay her tax and National Insurance under the PAYE scheme. This is an awful headache, and if you pay your nanny less than the minimum taxable earnings rate – currently £26.50 a week you may be able to avoid it. You will have to approach your local PAYE office – you will find them in the phone book under Inland Revenue – and ask them to advise you and let you have the necessary forms.

It is a very good idea to have a trial period of employment which could be anything from a week to a month. Make sure that you are around to begin with, so that your children can get used to her slowly in the security of your presence, and also so that you can watch and see how she behaves with them. If there is anything that you do not like, check it immediately; otherwise her faults will nag at you. If somebody turns out to be hopelessly unsuitable, grit your teeth and fire them. It is a horrible thing to do, but your children have to come first. It is no use hoping that matters might improve. If you do have to fire someone, give some hard thought to the part you played in the failure. Were you being too demanding, too tolerant, too unrealistic? Both of you should learn from the experience.

There are other ways of finding nannies. The idea of national advertising and grand agencies who charge large fees is quite beyond most women. Try putting a card in a newsagent's window, or your local neighbourhood centre, or in a local paper. One GP found the perfect grandmother substitute through an advertisement in a sweetshop window, and I have found a reservoir of baby-sitters through my local community centre. '*My ideal,*' said the GP, '*is to find someone who lives on the doorstep, who doesn't have children of her own so that they can't come in when their kids are ill. Basically I want a frustrated granny, a middle-aged sensible lady, and I got one who fitted the bill exactly. Then she had to leave and I've now got a lady who's had problems having children of her own and who's big and fat and motherly and just loves babies.*'

This kind of arrangement comes a lot cheaper than the fully qualified nanny and a great many mothers feel a lot more comfortable with it. There is one other solution that ought to be increasingly popular with young mothers who cannot afford a nanny all to themselves and that is the Share-a-Nanny scheme. This was started by the Nanny Service, but there is no reason why any two mothers should not get together, work out their needs and then hire a nanny between them to look after their two lots of children. Jane Reid explains how it works.

'*Share-a-Nanny mums have got to be flexible above all. It's for people who want a full-time day nanny at half price. We've now got about twenty to twenty-five successful shares working. We match up the mothers and the nanny and charge each mother half the fee. Now it's been going a little while we get women coming to us who are friends and have decided together that they want someone and that arrangement has a better chance of working. The trouble is that Share-a-Nanny mums often haven't done their homework. They have to agree to pay her salary whatever happens – if the partnership breaks up or one woman opts out then the nanny mustn't suffer. They'll come and say they want someone full-time except in the holidays, or they haven't worked out how the nanny will cope with children of different ages. They haven't worked out what kind of pram could accommodate a toddler and a baby and then combined to buy one. We have one pair working really well. One mother has a baby of eight months, the other has a child of a year, and they bought a double buggy between them. One mother brings her child into central London with her, where she works, and takes her to the other mother where the nanny looks after both of them.*'

A nanny or mother's help means a huge chunk out of your salary, but if you look at it from her point of view, she earns very little compared with what she could get working in a shop or an office. Luckily for the mothers who need them, it seems there will always be a supply or girls and women who simply love working with children and are not interested in working in offices. Your chances of finding such a person are highest apparently, in central London or in the real country. Nannies are happy to work in Wiltshire or Knightsbridge, but they don't want to know about Croydon or Gants Hill. The agencies I list at the end of the book are based in London but they will find people to work all over the country. You could also try your local paper or local employment agency, as well as *The Lady* and *Nursery World* whose addresses I also give.

Mothers of under-fives look forward joyfully to the days when their dependent children will be at school and their troubles – or the worst of them – will be over. Mothers of school children say they have only just begun. The provision of after-school and holiday care for children is even less and more difficult to find than the provision of day care for little children, and the kind of trouble that active, lively children on the loose can get into hardly bears thinking about. The accident rate for children shoots up in the hours immediately after the end of the school day when tired children make their way home, some of them to an empty house. Over a quarter of burn cases admitted to hospital are unsupervised children. Some mothers who were latch key children themselves and can vividly remember the loneliness and fear of coming home to an empty house, refuse, despite wanting to work, to turn their children into latch key children as well.

'I won't take work that affects my sons' lives,' wrote a Woman's Own reader. 'I myself was a latch key child, getting my own meals, being terrified of the empty house, standing with my back to the wall petrified until I heard the next person arriving home.'

'I was a latch key child from the age of eight,' wrote another. 'I would have to come home from school, light two fires, peel potatoes, get tea ready and lay a table, also look after my brother who was six years old. When I look back on it I think how disgusting it was, a working mother and no-one to look after the children. I have now got three children of my own. After my early years I haven't got the heart to go out to work and leave them to their own devices.'

A report produced by Robin Simpson for the Equal Opportunities Commission identified the core of the problem as the five to ten year olds. According to the 1971 census that means 2.72 million children. Official estimates say that 20% of five to ten years olds are left alone during the school holidays and 15% are alone after school. For 11 to 15 year olds the figures are 25% and

20%. This means that 675,000 school children are left alone in the school holidays and 525,000 are left alone after school. No wonder that four out of five mothers questioned for the *Woman's Own* survey wanted proper after-school care.

In the absence of organised care mothers resort to the same kind of threadbare patchwork that most of them relied on during the pre-school years. '*When my daughter started school,*' says a single mother, '*a relative took and collected her to and from school, but after a few weeks she could not do it any longer. Naturally I was frantic. I had lived in the area only five months and hardly knew anyone. So I asked the neighbour. I pay her £5 a week. The holidays are a nightmare. During the summer holidays I am allowed two weeks' holiday. The other four weeks my daughter spends at a friend's house. Because of the distance I have to take her there on a Sunday and collect her on a Friday. So for all her school holidays I will be a weekend Mum. I don't like it. I am constantly worried about the situation and I feel I cannot look too far into the future in case something goes wrong.*'

The biggest spanner in the works for mothers who have managed to set up this kind of perilous arrangement is the unpredictable behaviour of the schools, particularly if there are two or more school children in the family. Half-term holidays can be guaranteed to be on different days, and then there are other unaccountable problems as this student mother reports.

'*My two children, who are seven and nine, are at school until three thirty. On two days a week when I have lectures until five, I have to pay out of my slender grant for someone to meet them. Of course there are those days when the schools suddenly close because of a strike, or fuel shortage, an election, a teachers' extra day's holiday (three per year – the two schools never seem able to synchronise them, therefore six odd days off per year) and then there are half-term weeks. On all those occasions the children either have to come and sit quietly (two boys of seven and nine?) in a corner of the college while I attend classes, or I have to stay at home and try to catch up some other time.*'

Other mothers report worries over older school children whom they pay to collect their smaller children from school, and fallible arrangements with neighbours. Mothers who have forgone these uncertain arrangements in the hope that their children are mature enough to get home and look after themselves without trouble are constantly nagged by doubt, and as a secretary with two school age sons admitted, probably lose concentration towards the end of the afternoon as they wonder what their children are up to in their

85

absence, even if they make a deliberate effort to control their children's activities at a distance.

A mother in the Bermondsey study on working mothers arranged the day of her ten and six year old daughters during her absence. She kept them up late in the evening so that they would sleep until their father woke them up on his way to work at 7.30. They breakfasted off milk and cereal which their mother had set out for them. Then they told the lady in the next flat they were up and went off to a nearby playground until their mother got in at 12.30. The playground had a shelter in case it rained, but this cannot be the ideal arrangement.

If you have no choice but to leave your children to come home on their own, you can help your children's independence – and your own peace of mind – by a little elementary training and some basic ground rules. Insist that your children come straight home from school. If you have a phone and you are contactable at your work suggest that they check in by phone as soon as they get in. Don't let them use the cooker or play with any gas or electric appliances. Always leave a spare key with the neighbour in case they lose theirs. Don't let them have friends around while you are still at work – you cannot be responsible for other children in your absence. Leave them a cheering note and a snack to find when they get home. It will make the house seem less empty. And suggest activities they can carry out until you get home. Homework is the obvious answer but if the children have hobbies, they can be getting on with something to show you when you reach home, rather than wandering aimlessly about the place feeling neglected.

Most working mothers report an increase in their children's independence when both parents work, but don't push your children too hard too soon. Give them a little guidance. Make sure that they can cope on their own, don't trust to luck. If you know that you are going to be out at work over a period when they will be alone, start teaching them to cope in advance. Make sure that they know how to make a basic snack and can find their way on public transport alone. Give them an emergency drill in case anything drastic goes wrong. They should have the doctor's phone number and a selection of other people to contact if they need help. Make sure that the neighbours know they are there on their own, even if they do not do anything about it. Drill them in what to do if a stranger calls or if they lose their keys. Children will behave up to your expectations of them and it is possible for them to be aware of your caring presence and your rules even if you are actually somewhere else.

Lucky mothers do not have to cope with the problem of latch key children because they have an after-school scheme in their area or a good holiday play scheme for their children to go to. I say 'lucky', because not only are such schemes thin on the ground but they are difficult to find. School children whose parents both work can come under a wide range of official and unofficial provisions. There are local authority play schemes, often based in the school itself with special paid staff to run them. The Inner London Education Authority has a good record for after-school schemes and it provides places for 18,000 children to stay safely in school each evening with a range of activities to do. Numbers expand in the school holidays. There are voluntary play centres and supervised adventure playgrounds which can give your children a lot of fun, but do not act as substitute mother care. There is a small but growing number of special children's centres or children's houses like Gingerbread Corner which caters for up to 100 children each day and is open the whole time. And some day nurseries will accept an older brother of sister coming in to while away after-school and holiday times.

Unfortunately, all this raggle taggle provision comes under a wide variety of different organisations. Robin Simpson found that play schemes came under Education, under Social Services, under Leisure and Amenities, under Parks and even in one local authority, under the Borough Engineer. Apart from these local authority schemes the National Playing Fields Association keeps a register of 3,000 holiday play schemes but even this is not comprehensive. Nor is there any central register of after-school care. Part of the problem is that no single government department has a duty to provide care or education out of school hours or during school holidays and there is no obvious channel for getting funds for such schemes. Self-help groups who set up day care and holiday schemes have to trudge from one grant-making body to another in order to scrape funds together. Gingerbread Corner in Croydon, got their money from the EEC Poverty Fund. The Howgill Centre in Cumbria is supported by the Save The Children Fund and another Gingerbread Centre, Dove Centre, is funded by the Magdalen Hospital Fund.

These three schemes are good examples of what can be done when parents stir themselves to provide the facilities for their children themselves. If you want to know how to set about this, see the next chapter. The Dove Gingerbread Centre, for example, is based in an old school which not only houses the children's schemes but provides extra space for other community activities. There is a day nursery, an after-school and holiday centre for about 60 five to twelve year olds, and an advice and counselling centre for one parent families. Because one parent families have a more urgent need for help than two parent families, they have a good record of getting this kind of scheme off the ground fast.

The most celebrated example is the Gingerbread Corner in Croydon, an informal house which looks after the children of single parents both after school and in the holidays in a homely and friendly atmosphere. Fifty-four per cent of the Gingerbread Corner parents are in secretarial or clerical work and the rest are in comparatively low-grade jobs in industry, or students, caterers or cleaners; 28% said that the scheme had freed them to get a better job and 23% said it enabled them to work longer hours. In fact the average wage of these parents was low, around £2,849, which is a good indication of the way in which single parents are disadvantaged. But this freedom was not the only benefit. When the parents were asked what they thought the primary benefit of the Centre was to them and their families they replied 'peace of mind'. At last they are free from worry about how their children are cared for in their absence, they find it a way of meeting people and they also found that they and their children got along much better once the children attended the Centre and they were free to work.

If you want to find out about day care centres, after-school schemes and holiday schemes in your area the first place to try is the local education authority who will be able to tell you if any of the schools in your area operate such a scheme. Failing that, you could try the Social Services Department. If neither of these departments know of anything try asking for the Council Information Officer who should be able to find out for you if it comes under some other heading. Various groups produce lists of voluntary organised schemes and are concerned with campaigning strongly for the use of empty school buildings and equipment during the long summer holidays. You will find a list at the back of the book. If none of these can offer a scheme which would suit your children, then you may feel energetic enough to start your own. In the next chapter I tell you how.

9   Self-help Day Care

Working mothers have no time, but there are always some people who manage to treat their time like bubble gum. These are the people who get things done. These are the people who may have the energy and rage to fill in the gaps of the day care system for themselves and have a go at running their own nursery/after-school scheme/day care centre/ holiday scheme. I wish them all the luck in the world and I am happy to be able to tell them that a great fund of knowledge already exists on this very problem. The following brief account of how to set up a scheme of your own owes a great deal to Julie Kaufmann's excellent pamphlet *Self-Help Day Care Schemes* published by Gingerbread and available from Gingerbread at 35 Wellington Street, London WC2, price 95p. At the end of the book you will find a more comprehensive list of the literature produced by voluntary and official organisations to help people striking out on their own.

Anybody who wants to set about running their own child care scheme must be systematic and professional about it from the beginning. Stage One is to provide yourself with all the information you require to ensure that there is a need for the scheme you attempt to set up, and that you know how to meet it. Find out what provision there is already in your area. Then find out what the demand might be. Are there waiting lists for the facilities that exist? Circulate a questionnaire to people who are likely to be interested.

Once you have established a demand, set up a proper management structure. Give the people involved separate responsibilities, such as fund-raising, book-keeping, wages, premises, dealing with local authorities and drumming up publicity.

You need money, and there are hundreds of potential sources of this stuff. The trouble is that most trusts will not consider an application for a grant except from registered charities. In order to register as a charity you must apply to the Charity Commissioners, The Charity Commission, 14 Ryden Street, London SW1. Telephone 01-214 5000. It takes more than a letter to the Charity Commissioners to turn you into a registered charity. You must draw up a proper constitution which states clearly your aims and objectives, the need you think you can meet, your qualifications and interests. The Charity Commissioners will help you if you approach them first. You may also find that you need the services of a lawyer in order to word your application properly.

When you are looking for premises bear certain basic requirements in mind. They must be easily accessible to the maximum number of people in your own area. A central area of town or a large housing estate is a good place to begin looking. You may find old, purpose-built nurseries or schools closed down, or unused buildings on a school site. Approach the council to see if they have any empty houses. Try and get local councillors on your side. Beware of taking on a short-term lease because it may run out and leave you back where you started. Parents and money will not come to you unless there is a reasonable certainty that you can be relied upon to keep going for a decent length of time. Once you have found your premises, insure them against fire, theft, damage and accidents, and remember that charities are entitled to reductions in premiums.

You have to register with the local Social Services Department under the Nurseries and Child Minders Regulations Act as amended by the Health Service and Public Health Act of 1968. It is as well to get these people on your side as soon as possible so that you can incorporate their suggestions and advice into your plan. This also applies to the fire prevention officer. Social Services officers will advise you on the ratio of staff to children, on the necessary space per child, on the basic kitchen facilities you need, on the basic heating requirements, on the provision of toilet and washing facilities and access to outside play space. Like childminders, nursery or day care staff have to have a yearly chest X-ray and sign the eligibility form which says they were never prosecuted under the Children and Young Persons Act.

It is essential for the success of a long-term venture to have paid staff, although running a staff brings its own problems such as grievances over pay and conditions, and personality clashes. The

91

children themselves may have problems you will have to deal with. It is essential to keep the phone number of a child's GP in case of emergencies and to be alert to potential unhappiness when a new child is settling in.

Once your project is off the ground you have to consider how to fund it. If you charge fees to parents you will want to keep them as low as possible and you may want to consider grants from other sources.

If you are aiming to supply a stopgap scheme for after school and school holidays then you are not so subject to red tape as you are for full-time day care. Approach local schools for their support and draw up a questionnaire for children to take home to their parents. This will help you to gauge the need for such a scheme. If any of the head teachers seem sympathetic to the idea, then try them first with the use of the school premises. Once your scheme has got going never turn anybody away out of hand. Keep a waiting list as evidence of the continuing need for the service you offer.

Part Three
Working Mothers and Work

10   Getting Ready to Jump

I think it was Margaret Drabble who said that married women were the last class of society to benefit from an unearned income. Actually, we earn every penny we get whether we go out to work to get it or receive it from our husbands. But she made a valuable point. Unless your income is absolutely vital to the survival of the family, you, as a married woman with an earning husband can exercise some freedom of choice over, not only whether you work or not, but over what you work at and when. There is not yet the same kind of pressure on women as there is on men to sink everything into their careers and keep climbing the promotion ladder, or to do more and more overtime. If a man decided to give up work for five years society would look askance. If a woman does it when she has children, it is considered not only normal but admirable.

This freedom to be flexible is one of the few advantages which women enjoy, and it may reconcile you to your time spent at home if you think of it as a rejuvenating and retraining period for work. Even if you do not give up work completely, this is a period which you can use to reassess yourself and to think about what you want to do with the rest of your life.

An American study on working mothers pointed out that American men typically suffer a crisis of doubt about their careers in their mid-thirties, whereas American working mothers had already come to terms with their own balance between ambition and family. Women have to make room in their lives for human values which is one reason why they often have a more relaxed attitude to their jobs. Even quite successful and high-achieving women can see the advantage of slowing down their careers when their children most need them. A professor quoted in a study brought up her three sons single-handed and was quite happy to spend more time in her life ducking promotion and work pressures in their favour. *'When you're forced to make daily decisions about how you're spending your time,'* she said, *'you have to stop and ask "is my career important to me because I want to be working so hard right now, or is it because everyone else says I ought to be?"'*

Women in Top Jobs, a British study, found that *'women are more likely than men to be interested in balancing family or leisure interests against work and to settle for a satisfying job which leaves room for this rather than drive towards the peaks of a profession. Women, that great majority of them who marry and have children, do need to be treated as a class in respect of the timing of their careers. The pressures to slow down or drop out are severe. One senior woman described how she planned her career so that while her children were small she deliberately kept herself in a backwater, doing a job that was well within her capabilities.'*

The fact is that if you want a balanced life, as many women do, then it takes some planning and forethought. A child-rearing break from work may be the ideal time to think the whole thing over again but the best time to think about being a working mother is before you are one.

There are two approaches to combining a career with motherhood. One is to build up your career first, get good qualifications and a solid grounding of experience and reputation before retiring. This means that you should be in a good position to break back into the job market when you decide to return. The other approach is to rush the marriage and babies and save your working life until the intensive domestic period is over. This second strategy is more difficult to plan. Unfortunately you can not go out and pick up a husband and children the way you can hunt for a job. So the sooner you can get started on making yourself employable, the less time you waste all round, whether you intend to have children or not. The far-sighted girl can even look, in advance, for work that is particularly compatible with motherhood – work that can be done freelance at home or educational work that fits in with school holidays. Don't, whatever you do, say to yourself 'I don't need any qualifications because I'm only going to get married anyway.' That is a trap which leaves you with no control over your own life. You may find yourself in the unhappy situation of this *Woman's Own* reader who tentatively started to look for simple work after a gap of ten years at home. She had no qualifications and no self-confidence.

'A few weeks ago I went for an interview for an afternoon job. I know I didn't stand much of a chance because of my weak eyes, but this didn't really

bother me. But it was a fact that after ten years I was expected to remember the names of my employers so that they could get references. This was impossible. Two of them were dead and the other one had moved address. I felt rather depressed after failing this interview. I even considered what I know I can do – have another baby. But for a good friend I was talked out of it so I am building up my confidence to try again.'

Don't get into a situation where all you can think of doing is having another baby. What could be sadder? When you do leave work to have your baby, if you do decide to leave, don't forget that you will want to get back in one day. Collect your references as you leave. Keep in, if at all possible, with your colleagues and bosses. You will need to know them in the future when you are looking for work again. If you belong to a trade union or a professional body, keep up your membership and be flexible, too, about the period when you put your family before your work. Some women prefer to work while the children are babies and take time off at a later stage when the children more actively need their company, conversation and advice.

If having a baby coincides with a peak in your career then you will either have to neglect the children, forgo the peak, or push yourself to the limits of your endurance to keep everybody happy. You may have to do some fast rethinking. High-powered women workers with a secure place in the job market even owe it to their sisters to do a little pioneering. If you do mean to stay at work even while your children are small and if you are ambitious in the long term and know you are a valued member of a team, then try to keep working on your own terms. Point out that for the time being you have to balance your work with intensive family responsibilities but that you do not want to be shelved altogether. Say that you are willing to take a back seat for a little while, even though you do not want to be overlooked for training or future promotion when you are ready to put more energy back into the job. It sounds radical, but until women start trying to mould the world of work to take account of the family, it will never change. Above all, don't be apologetic. And don't be afraid to turn down a good work opportunity. If you have anything to you, there will be more, and this one could misfire on you if you take on more than you can handle.

If you are a well-qualified professional who has the confidence to plan out a career which takes account of your family too, then you don't need my advice. But a very large number of women work in a desultory sort of way before their marriage, give up when they have children and then find, a stretch of maybe twenty years ahead of them, that they have no qualifications, no experience of any great value in the job market and no confidence at all. It is possible that their mothers were equally unqualified and un-career minded. Career adviser Ruth Miller found that *'mothers didn't seem to connect cause (little training and career planning) and effect (bored after 35).'* Even if you did have a reasonable job before you left work, it is quite likely in today's fast changing job market that you may find a reduced demand for your services in that particular area when you want to return.

So how can you best use this enforced period of retrenchment? The first thing you need to do – and motherhood will be helping you a lot – is to find out more about yourself. What kind of a person are you? What activities do you most enjoy? What tasks do you do most competently? What areas bore you to death? Without any great commitment of time or money you can test yourself in various ways. If a subject interests you, go to a regular evening class and see if it was just a passing fancy or whether you have real ability. More women than men do go to evening classes but they tend to take domestic, uncommercial subjects like flower arranging. They do not think of them as a way to advance their careers. If you have no qualifications, look at the enormous amount of correspondence courses available to you. If you lack skills, there are all kinds of things you can teach yourself at home with books and cassettes.

Look at the kind of unpaid work which is open to women based at home. Join or help to set up a local playgroup and then take advantage of the various playgroup leader courses. Volunteer your services at the local Social Services Department or to the WRVS or the community centre or your local hospital. Not only is the work you could be doing interesting and valuable, it also provides you with experience which any future employer would take into account, and would broaden your ideas on the kind of work you might like to do later.

CAREERS GUIDANCE

If you feel you need professional guidance in evaluating your job potential, there is a wide range of career counselling services and a limitless number of publications on careers which will give you all the information you could possibly want. A proper careers counselling session is aimed at finding out more about you through questionnaires and aptitude tests and personal interviews. The counsellor will then be able to tell you that you hate people, do not mind domestic tasks such as cleaning up or preparing food, like animals and the unexpected and might be well advised to consider taking an assistant keeper's job in the local zoo. Many careers guidance services are privately run and charge a substantial fee – usually at least £25–50. If you want a free assessment, the first place to go is your local Job Centre or Government run employment exchange, who will tell you where to find the nearest Occupational Guidance Unit or failing a nearby Occupational Guidance Unit, will arrange an interview with a careers officer.

Once you know what kind of job you might be suited for you are in a position to narrow your search. You want to know what job opportunities exist in your area for people with your special combination of qualifications and personal aptitudes. Here again a careers guidance counsellor should be able to help you, and the advice they may give you could come as a shock. The 1980s are going to bring about radical changes in the job market which will mostly affect women. Computers and micro-processors will do away with many of the jobs which have been traditionally filled by women. The TUC estimates that about 1½ million out of the current 3½ million clerical workers will be out of a job in the next ten years. In banking and insurance alone some 200,000 women are threatened by unemployment. All the tedious routine work of commerce can be handled by computer.

But there is no need to be downcast by the micro-chip revolution. According to the TUC, in the future all workers may have to change jobs several times during their lives, with periods for retraining in between. This is a pattern which may suit women very well and put them at less of a disadvantage in the job market. A lot of jobs will go, but they were the undemanding, unrewarding jobs anyway. And it may hasten an overdue realisation by women that if they want interesting and well-paid work then they should wrench their brain to think about the kind of work that men traditionally do. If you want to sell, goes one piece of brisk advice, don't sell dresses, sell cars; don't sell shoes, sell insurance,; don't run the typing pool, run the factory. If you want to escape from the low-paid, low-opportunity trap into which most women fall then start thinking more like a man.

The areas in which there will be new jobs in the future are the technological and scientific fields, and women are being actively encouraged to join them. The Engineering Training Board, for example, has started to give fifty annual undergraduate awards for women entering engineering degree courses and 250 grants to women training as technicians. The micro-chip revolution is creating a need for people to run and service it, for programmers and technicians and systems analysts. And it is not even necessary to think of yourself as a scientist and technician to be eligible for some of this work. Apparently people with language ability make the best computer programmers because it involves translation from one language into another – computer talk. Even the traditional female job of secretary will become more interesting and responsible as the routine is taken out of it and an element of research and data sifting creeps in.

If you already have a vocation and a training – you may, for example, be a nurse – consider expanding it. Take a specialised course and promote yourself. In fact, once you have homed-in on an area of work which interests you, there is no limit to the choice of courses, retraining and further education open to you. The better qualified you are the better your chance of getting a decent job, particularly if you take a vocational course – a course undertaken with a particular job in mind – and you know in advance that you will be able to find work once you are qualified.

Before you jump in, you may be able to attend one of a number of courses which are run throughout the country under the general title of 'New Opportunities for Women' or 'Wider Opportunities for Women'. Two places which run these courses are Hatfield Polytechnic, in Hertfordshire and the University of Newcastle-upon-Tyne Department of Adult Education. New Opportunities for Women courses are designed, according to one of the brochures, to act as *'A comprehensive guide to the mature woman who may wish to return to an active working life but is unsure or unaware of how best to do so.'* NOW courses are designed to help their students to find out about all the opportunities there are for re-education, part-time or full-time jobs, second careers or voluntary services. One of their happiest effects is to restore lost self-confidence and to introduce the people who attend them to others in the same boat. They tell students how to polish up their skills or improve the qualifications they already hold and how to plan out a long-term career, taking into account each student's special interests and abilities and home circumstances.

The courses are built up of lectures, talks from potential employers and interested government agencies, aptitude and personality tests and a personal consultation for each student with specially trained careers counsellors. At best a student can leave a NOW course with a clear idea of what she wants to do with her life and how to go about it. At its most basic level, the course can boost her morale and clarify her mind, even if she still decides to stay at home after all.

The Professional and Executive Recruitment of the Department of Employment also runs 'Return to Work' courses for which you may be eligible. The Training Opportunities Scheme or TOPS which functions mainly as a retraining agency also runs 'Back to Work' courses specifically aimed at people who were, or are, at managerial or professional level before they decided to switch careers. This is a good example of why it is wise to get as well qualified as possible before you drop out. The more qualified you are when you stop, the wider the range of opportunity open to you when you start again.

These Career Development Conferences, as they are called, are aimed at helping the redundant executive as much as returning professional women but they are run as two-week residential courses with a weekend break. They include career information, career planning, confidence restoring and discussion. People who attend them have their fees paid by the Manpower Services Commission. You can apply to attend these courses through the Professional and Executive Recruitment although they are separate from the Professional and Executive Recruitment's own career and job-hunting seminars and self-presentation courses. You can get information on all these courses from the TOPS adviser at your local Job Centre. If you want to find out if this kind of course is available near you, you can approach your local technical college or university, or your local education authority. Or you can write to a central body which is involved in running courses, such as TOPS or the Manpower Services or the National Advisory Council on Careers for Women.

VOCATIONAL TRAINING

If you want to qualify yourself for a specific job, maybe for a kind of work you have never done before, you are the ideal candidate for a TOPS course. TOPS stands for Training Opportunities Scheme, and a TOPS course not only retrains you in a specific, marketable skill, it pays you while you do your training. The basic TOPS course allowance is currently £27.75 a week if you are living at home or £24.05 a week plus a lodgings allowance or residential accommodation if you need to study away from home. You get travelling expenses over two miles, free midday meals or an allowance and an earnings-related supplement if you have been working and are not self-employed. The TOPS allowance is tax-free. In order to qualify for the TOPS grant the course you do must lead directly to a job and it must last for between one and 12 months. You are eligible if you are over 19, unemployed or willing to give up your present job, if you intend to take up work with your new skills and if you have been away from full-time education for at least three years. If you have a family and are in strained circumstances you may also be eligible for Family Income Supplement, rent and rates rebate and certain benefits for your children, such as free school meals.

There are two ways in which to approach TOPS courses; one is to look at the selection of TOPS courses available to you at your local education centre and choose one. The TOPS courses are essentially in practical subjects and before they decide to take you on, you will be asked to do an aptitude test. There is no point in deciding to do a course on painting and decorating if you turn out to have a vertigo at the top of the ladder or are colour blind. The TOPS booklet lists the following selection of skills and they are very emphatic that women can do any of them: bricklaying, plastering, plumbing, painting and decorating, carpentry, joinery, electrical installation, masonry, heating engineering, radio and TV repair, shorthand and typing, hotel catering, hotel reception, baking, watch and clock repairing, hairdressing, retailing and wholesaling, and boat outfitting. And that is just a tiny selection of what is available. You can do these courses at any one of sixty Skill Centres or at a wide range of technical colleges and specialised centres throughout the country.

The other way is to decide what you would like to do, find

somewhere that will teach it to you, produce some evidence that you will be employed if you are qualified and then apply to TOPS for a grant to do the course. One enterprising woman did this by deciding she wanted to attend a private interior decorating school. She produced some letters from clients who promised to employ her if she took the course, and, she got her grant.

FURTHER EDUCATION

If you decide to go further, you can take an academic course such as an external degree or an Open University course, or you can join a vocational retraining course. If you are interested in becoming better educated without undertaking a course which has a particular job waiting for you at the end of it, you can either study at home – something which may suit your domestic situation but which requires an enormous amount of self-discipline and hard work – or you can attend a college. There are several adult education colleges around the country which specialise in teaching adults who do not have a background of higher education. If you can arrange to attend an adult education college you would be eligible to undertake a two year course leading to university-recognised diplomas or certificates, mainly in social sciences and liberal arts fields. There are several of these colleges for mature students but two of them in particular are aimed at helping women. One is for women only: Hillcroft College, South Bank, Surbiton, Surrey. The other pays special attention to women and goes as far as to provide whole family accommodation and a crèche. This is Norther College, Wentworth Castle, Stainborough, Barnsley, Yorkshire. Some of its courses are for ten weeks or less.

The Open University is a natural choice for lots of people who would like to study at home. It offers a relatively wide selection of courses; you can take the degree course at your own pace and you do not have to have any educational qualifications to qualify as a student. Fees are payable but there is a hardship fund for students who really cannot afford to study. To find out more about the Open University write for their *Guide to Applicants*. If you feel you need more detailed guidance than this, in particular about fees, you can ask for a personal interview with an Open University counsellor.

Another body which can advise you on a range of educational correspondence courses to degree level is the National Extension College, 18 Brooklands Avenue, Cambridge CB2 2AJ, which operates its own student advisory service. The University of London runs a wide external degree programme and further information is available from Senate House, Malet Street, London WC1 7AQ.

To find out more about of these courses I suggest you send for a very useful booklet called *Second Chance Education* written by Ruth Miller for *Good Housekeeping* and available from them.

GRANTS

Retraining takes one thing that many housebound mothers do not have and that is money. It is quite possible that you may qualify for a grant to follow your chosen course, depending on its level. If you want to go to your local technical college and take some more GCE examinations, you do not qualify for a grant. But once you get further up the scale then you do. Degree courses and courses at residential adult education colleges automatically qualify for a grant. And if you are doing a TOPS course you are eligible for a TOPS grant. To find out more about grants and where to obtain them, consult a Department of Education guide called *Grants for Students,* contact the National Union of Students Grants adviser or, in Scotland, The Scottish Education Department. If you want more general information on further education, write to the Higher Education Advisory Centre.

Going back to work is a big step. It is hard for people who stay in the working world to understand how quickly a woman confined to children and domestic routine can lose her self-confidence and sparkle. There are thousands of women in the same position as you, and all the official bodies who are concerned with higher education and retraining are putting themselves out more and more to help you. Once you have made the first difficult step it gets easier, and more exciting and stimulating. Before you know it you will find yourself applying for a job.

11   Mothers Versus Employers

A mother went to an employment agency and asked for a part-time job that would give her time off during the school holidays. They laughed sardonically. '*Just like all the other mothers*,' they said, as they showed her the door. Apart from the dedicated or the desperate few, most mothers dream of the job that will allow them the time and the emotional energy to look after their families. This weakness is easily detected and exploited by the world of employers. While highly qualified and professional women with a good reputation can ease themselves back into work, or cope with clients from home or attend their offices only on certain days a week, there is a kind of mug's law that says the more desperately you need part-time work the more you have to pay for it in terms of low pay, low job protection, low responsibility, low chances of promotion and low security.

Mothers who do try to find work that will fit in with their families soon find out the realities of life, like this *Woman's Own* reader who works part-time as a night auxiliary nurse and looks after her six and seven year old girls during the day. '*Before I got this job five months ago,*' she said, '*I did all the usual things – factory home work (boring and frustrating), Avon lady (interesting meeting people but very little pay and out, kids and all, in all weather and no future) and a cleaning job (poor pay and no interest – all the things one has to do at home, but I could take the children with me). I don't believe in leaving children on their own. I think Mum is tremendously important in their lives, this is why I got night work. I also don't believe in giving up one's own self and living only through one's family.*'

There's the dilemma. How do you find the kind of job that satisfies you and also takes your responsibilities as a mother into account? A *Sunday Times* survey found that most women preferred to work near their homes so that they could be near their families, preferred work that slotted in with family life, and preferred work that was enjoyable and friendly to work that was well paid.

Flexibility is all. This need to combine flexibility with a basic living wage often means that a woman will end up juggling a number of part-time jobs. One mother taught English to foreign students, washed up in a lodging house and worked as a night nurse. Another did an evening job in a pub and a Saturday job in a shop while her husband was home. But even work that is part-time can be a full-time emotional commitment. Not being in your place of work does not stop you worrying about it, or having to cope with the responsibility, any more than not being at home stops you worrying about your children.

Mothers are prepared to give up a lot to have the advantages of part-time work. If you work less than 21 hours a week you are not entitled to sickness or holiday pay, and in most cases, no job protection or paid maternity leave. If you do temporary freelance work, as a secretary, for example, the work is unpredictable and inclined to fluctuate. And rates of pay for both part-time and temporary workers are lower than for full-time workers.

Whatever kind of work mothers look for, they may be shocked to find that in a prospective employer's eyes they have one huge drawback – their children. Having children can down-grade qualified women and put unqualified ones out of the job market altogether. A qualified telephonist says she has given up going for interviews for telephonist work because every employer she has ever been interviewed by makes it clear that he would rather have a person without a child at school. An experienced secretary wrote to *Woman's Own* to say that she is now working as an evening shift office cleaner.

'*I've done this job for nearly one year and before that I tried unsuccessfully for many months to get a job as a secretary (I had a childminder lined up). All the interviews I attended, and there were many, went well until I revealed that I had two children under school age. Then I got the same old story. "Won't it be difficult for you to work with children so young?" What rubbish. I had made arrangements with a very good and reliable childminder who knew my two children well. I am qualified and willing to work but I am discriminated against because I have children.*'

It seems that a large number of employers either want a cast iron guarantee that child care is completely organised or they fight shy of mothers altogether. Careers advisers suggest that a mother going for a job interview should be prepared with answers to the following questions. Do you have adequate day care arrangements for your children? Who will look after them if they are ill or on holiday? Can you cope with the stress of doing this job and running a family? Others advise that you do not mention the children at all, and a lot of mothers do manage to keep their motherhood a secret from their employer. But why should you have to resort to subterfuge and lies? Employers' attitudes will never change until they realise that working mothers are a fact of life and that most of them are reliable. The absentee rates of mothers are no higher than anyone else's. Being a mother is nothing to be apologetic about. In fact there is one point of view which maintains that mothers try harder, simply because they are so conscious of having to prove themselves reliable.

You may have to fight, like the qualified hospital receptionist who applied for the same job three times. She was short-listed each time, but each time the selection committee told her that they were unhappy about her family responsibilities. And the job went to somebody else. Each time it fell vacant again – presumably because the non-mother they chose proved to be unreliable – and each time she reapplied. The third time she got so furious with the whole business that she wrote the selection committee a stiff letter accusing them of discrimination and pointing out that she was obviously the best person for the job because of her experience and qualifications. This time they accepted her. Are you prepared to be that assertive? However you act in this situation, you should be aware of the fact that no man is ever asked what arrangements he has made for the care of his children, or whether he can cope with the strain of doing the job and having responsibility for his family. You may share the bewilderment of the mother who applied for a part-time job in a local hospital and was asked '*several times if, when the children were ill, I would still come in for work, which is surely illegal now as he wouldn't have asked the same question of a man. I didn't get the job, of course.*'

Strictly speaking it *is* illegal but nobody has yet been able to prove it. There may be a Sex Discrimination Act. Sex discrimination may, theoretically, be a thing of the past. But the realities of life are that all workers are equal but that some are more equal than others.

Let's look at what women actually do. The Department of Employment reported that two and a half million women were clerical workers, two million were employed in service industries, one million were teachers and nurses, and just under a million work in shops. Four out of ten workers are women but one third of these women work part-time compared with one twentieth of the male work force, and 87% of these part-time women workers are married. Only 12% of professional workers are women. We do have a woman Prime Minister. There are women in the Stock Exchange and in the Institute of Directors but the facts are that the vast majority of women do part-time, unskilled work.

One study of women part-time workers found that 67% of part-time married women were in unskilled or semi-skilled employment, working as domestic cleaners, canteen helpers, office cleaners, clerical workers and shop assistants. A book for single parents advises mothers to look for work as bar maids, late shift factory workers, waitresses, hotel maids, cinema usherettes, baby-sitters, factory and office cleaners or to make up personal mixtures of odd jobs. It is a very different picture from the one you get from the careers pages of a glossy women's magazine.

The introduction of the Sex Discrimination Act has done very little to change this dismal pattern. A Department of Employment study into occupational segregation between men and women reported a particularly gloomy picture of no change. Far from greater equality between the sexes at work, it found a complete stalemate, *'no strong and consistent trend over the century towards greater integration of the sexes in the work sphere. The results suggest rather that the small inroads made by women into "typically male" occupations may have led to the idea that significant changes have occurred in the pronounced division of the labour force into male and female occupations but the picture is broadly one of* little or no change since the turn of the century. *An increase in the number of women entering the labour force does not necessarily mean that they carry out a wider range of functions within it. Women increasingly form the majority of the labour force in the lowest grades of white collar and blue collar work. Often in occupations that closely mirror functions carried out on an unpaid and non specialist basis in the home.'*

Another study into the effects of the Sex Discrimination Act found that the position of women at work was almost entirely unaffected although it found what it considered to be a *'few small but potentially important changes. In four organisations a handful of women moved into traditionally male jobs, usually porter, engineering apprentice, engineer. A larger number of men moved into women's jobs in two organisations. A number of men applied for jobs as electronic assemblers, passed the dexterity tests and now comprised a third of operatives who were previously all female.'* Is that a victory for women?

The law may have been changed, but the main actors in it – women and employers – have not learnt any new lines. Until they do, women will be no better off. Women are largely unambitious, lacking in confidence, afraid to put themselves forward, too grateful for small mercies (especially if they have families). Employers think smugly that they are abiding by the Sex Discrimination Act when all they have done is change the wording of their job advertisements. The same old prejudices and the same old patterns of promotion still combine, furtively, to keep women in their place.

Employers traditionally think that women are unreliable (not only is this unproven, but older women have a more stable job record than young men). They think that boring, repetitive, meticulous jobs are particularly suitable for women. They can see for themselves that women are not political about their work in the same way that men are. Although women are well represented among trade union members, very few women ever get to be trade union officials, or even bother to attend meetings. *'If a woman can never get to a Union meeting because she has children to look after,'* suggests an NCCL pamphlet, *'then the care of those children should be something for the Union to worry about as well as the woman.'*

Training procedures inside firms have not changed so that women are not often offered the kind of educational and promotional opportunities that their male colleagues get, simply because managers assume that they are not interested, and women are usually too diffident to put themselves forward. Such training as there is, is often aimed at the youngest members of the team so that the older woman coming back to work after an absence looking after children automatically misses out. It is really up to women to push their employers further. There are decades of prejudice about women among managers. And not until female employees start putting themselves forward for promotion, applying for extra training or more demanding jobs will management begin to realise that their women workers should be taken seriously. And these women should be supported by their unions.

So there are three very important points that women have to impress on their employers. The first is that they take their work seriously. The second is that they take their families seriously. And the third is that it is quite possible to do both without either suffering. If the woman is very lucky, she can put herself one jump ahead by working for employers who *do* understand and who already make some allowances for their working mothers. One mother reports slaving herself to the bone in gratitude because her employer allows working mothers to take unpaid leave during the summer holidays. '*I later found that 165 women had applied for this job. I would think that any company who employs a woman on similar conditions to mine with children under 16, gets a good deal because one is conscientious to a fault, so grateful are you to have a job that fits in with school hours and holidays.*'

It also helps if you work for a woman who has children of her own so that she is understanding about the pressures under which you operate, though other women recommend a man with a working wife as being the better bet.

'*It helps to have a boss who understands,*' says one mother with a pre-school daughter. '*Mine pays lip service to the idea that a family is important but you can see that she really doesn't understand. The other morning I was late because I took my little girl to nursery and she didn't really want to go in, so I sat outside with her in the car and cuddled her and we took our time about and it turned out that a little girl had hit her the day before. So it was important that I spend that time with her. I wasn't going to rush into the office and leave her.*'

Some firms allow their employees a limited number of days off for school holidays and children's illness, either with or without pay. Check on this kind of arrangement at your interview – and hope that you are not dealing with the kind of employers who prefer not to employ mothers at all. And look out for the increasing number of staggered hour and job-sharing arrangements that can help a working mother combine all the work she has to do at home with doing a normal job.

Ask if the firm operates flexitime. This means that each employee ends up working a set number of hours each week, but it is up to them to choose what time to start in the morning and what time to leave in the evening. If you have to take your children to school, for example, you might prefer to work a day that starts at 9.30 rather than 9.00 and to finish later. You might prefer to skip your lunch hour, eat a sandwich at your desk and knock off at 4.00 p.m. in time to collect them. Or you might find a job with the kind of firm which allows you to cram your working week into four long days. This means that you lead a fairly hectic life for your working week but that you have three clear days to spend with your family and organise your domestic life.

The other growing practice which would suit working mothers much better than traditional working hours is job-sharing. In some rare cases husband and wife have been known to take on one job and split it between them, with the non-working partner looking after the children while the working partner goes off to work. But you do not have to turn into a husband and wife double act. Banks, in particular, have pioneered job-sharing and teaching is another area where it seems to work particularly well. In one case, two women teachers shared a job and the child care. One mother went to work in the morning while the other looked after both sets of children. They met at lunch time to arrange the hand over of work and discuss the particular project they were teaching. Then the second mother went off to school and the partner looked after the children for the afternoon.

It is possible to go to a prospective employer and ask if they have half a job. But it is a much better idea to find a job-sharing partner first, then apply for the job jointly. I know one specialist teacher who desperately wanted to unload her crowded week so that she had more time for her children and the ever un-done housework. She found someone who was happy to do two days of her teaching each week. They approached the education authority together. The education authority agreed and everybody was satisfied.

Unless women begin to take more control over their conditions of work – and enlist the support of their husbands – traditional, rigid, un-family minded working patterns will persist unchanged. Men have always had a right to choose careers and have children. You have that right too, but you will have to bend the rules to suit yourself. Once employers realise that the same amount and the same quality of work can get done, however unorthodox the arrangement, then more will have been done to give women equality of opportunity at work than has been achieved by any equal opportunities act.

12   Being Your Own Boss

When doom watchers are not predicting that we will all be turned into robots or made unemployed by the micro-chip revolution, they like to picture a universal, irresistible return to grass roots self-sufficiency. Everybody who is not plugged in to a computer will be beavering feverishly from sunrise to sunset, digging their own plot of ground, weaving their own clothes, rearing chickens and children indiscriminately. Either the future is all technology or it is all peasantry. Peasantry is what mothers used to be good at, and the idea of homely self-sufficiency, or at least home-based cottage industry has a very strong appeal.

Whatever the charms of cottage industry, and they are considerable, mothers who are thinking of abandoning job hunting and combining work and family in the one place, should clear their misty eyes and look at a few facts. If you have small children, working at home does not solve the problem of child care unless you need no sleep and can work entirely at night – or if your job is so mindless that it needs no concentration at all. It is absolutely impossible to get on with any sort of work in a business-like manner with children around, and that includes everything from washing dishes to writing a doctoral thesis.

The washing dishes can be interrupted without you or they suffering, but any kind of professional work needs uninterrupted concentration. It is also very unbusiness-like and off-putting to have telephone conversations about work while children or babies are yelling for attention. Nothing gives a quicker, more indelible impression of inefficiency than a baby crying in the background or one of those 'yes certainly . . . put it down, . . . Monday morning did you say? . . . Don't you dare . . . of course, no problem . . . oh my God, not on Mummy's best rug . . .' conversations which happen all too frequently.

Once your children start going to school then you will have clear time to yourself and the advantages of working from home will be reinforced. You do not necessarily need a full working week. One stupendously best-selling writer began her saga of love and war in the two mornings a week that her children spent at playgroup. Working at home saves a lot of time and money. You don't have to travel anywhere. You don't have to pay fares or petrol (though you do use up lighting and heat and endless jars of coffee). You will be on hand to cope with any family emergencies as and when they occur. Your children will find you there when they come home from school. You can draw up the balance of home and outside work that suits you best. But there are many pitfalls too. You can be all too easily distracted from work, whether by the need to make another cup of coffee or tidy up a corner that catches your eye, or dealing with the gas man, or by all those infuriating people who will assume that because you are at home you can't be working and must have all the time in the world for a long conversation, or a coffee, or for minding their child while they nip off to the post office. Not the least of these time wasters may be your husband.

'*When I was working full time in an office,*' reported one freelance mother, '*we split everything. But as soon as I started working at home he didn't lift a finger. He'd sit at the table and let me cook and bring in the food and clear it away and I began to think "there's something wrong here". He'd say "can you book these tickets? Or take this coat to the cleaners?" as though I had nothing else to do.*'

None of these people would treat you so casually if you were at the office. You have to learn to be tough enough to make it clear that at certain hours your home becomes office or factory and it is subjected to the same rules and regulations. And you must treat it like an office yourself. Don't keep leaping up to tidy the cushions.

'*Once I started working at home,*' continued the freelance journalist, '*I had to tidy up before starting work. I felt incessantly guilty. I could see clothes unfinished, shoes needing mending, everything just haunting me, whereas before I just used to close the door on them all. The household side of things left undone worries me, and there are constant interruptions when you work at home. It was all an awful shock. I now feel great compassion for people working at home who can't cope with deadlines, whereas I never used to understand before. People don't respect the fact that you're working, whereas the office is a formal working environment and people respect it.*'

Working at home can be claustrophobic and lonely, so if you work for companionship and the stimulation of other people, then it may not be for you. On the other hand, taking in lodgers or running a small hotel may provide you with more company than you can cope with. Self-employment which combines production at home with a mixture of outings – to deliver your projects and take orders for example – may provide an ideal balance. The greatest charm, for working mothers, is the way in which you can be in complete control of the balance of your own life. One dress designer who keeps production deliberately small, despite temptation to expand, does it because she thinks she has now got the balance absolutely right for her.

'*I got to the point where I make a living and I can't see the advantage in expanding. If I took on a shop or a small factory the over heads would rule out any extra income. This fits entirely with one's own life, it allows one to be free to do all the other things, reading and travelling, and I can't think of another job which would be so rewarding or which wouldn't involve day care or nannies for the children.*'

Some people think they will get rich and certainly nobody ever became rich working for an employer. Some people *do* get rich but most self-employed people put a higher value on the more intangible prize of freedom: freedom to make your own decisions and your own mistakes, freedom to work twenty hours at a stretch, freedom to knock yourself out for two months and then take school holidays off, freedom to say "*the hell with it*" and take the baby to the park instead.

But in the search for this freedom, there is one pitfall that every woman should beware of, and avoid at all costs. This is the home work trap. It is exploitation of the most degrading and depressing kind and it is almost entirely women who suffer from it. Women are particularly vulnerable because they need work they can do at home when they have children, and those worst off need it most. There are supposed to be over a quarter of a million home workers in this country doing piece work for outside employers at Dickensian rates of pay. In 1977 the TUC reported that they were earning between £10 and £15 for a thirty to forty hour week, about a quarter of the average earnings of women in full-time employment, and women's rates, as you will see in the next chapter, are much lower than the average rates for men. It is very nice to write a best seller on the kitchen table and earn a hundred thousand pounds. It is not at all nice to cut coat linings at 30p an hour or glue cheap toys for a pound a hundred. '*I did home work for a few months,*' said one mother, '*which was putting the backs on earrings, the clip-it-on sort. I had to do a thousand just to earn about £3. I would sit up half the night and they made your fingers bleed they were so rough.*'

The fact that working from home is the only kind of work that many women, particularly immigrants, can do, is exploited by their employers and unaffected by political protest. Local authorities are supposed to register all home workers, but there is no central record. The work is hazardous to health and can be dangerous to the children in the house. Industrial sewing machines may be installed in the living room, glue and paint and varnish can be left lying around. A report by Lyn Owen in *The Guardian* says that most home workers never see the factory which delivers them their work, so they never see the minimum rates of pay which employers are legally obliged to stick up on the factory wall. They receive little or no training from their employers and, of course, they receive none of the protections of factory work such as insurance, sick pay or holidays. Because they have no contract with the employer they get no job protection although they could, if they chose, fight this with a fair chance of winning.

Because in some cases their work in residential premises could be considered illegal and because they are frightened of the income tax authorities, most home workers do not want to attract attention to themselves and do not challenge their conditions of employment. The TUC would like to see home work banned altogether, not improved, although improving rates of pay and conditions would have the effect of making it unattractive to prospective employers and might help to phase it out. If you are attracted by advertisements for this kind of work, bear in mind that it is nothing but toil and drudgery for a negligible reward.

Apart from the underground home working industry there are two main approaches to working at home for money. One is for people who simply want to earn money in their spare time. The other is for professional, organised women who want to set up their own business. The first approach is enough to satisfy many women who want to feel useful, who want to earn some spare money and who want to have an outside interest in life. There are two very useful publications which will help you if you want to exploit the resources of your house and garden or make a hobby into something more profitable. One is a Consumer Association book called *Earning Money at Home*. The other is the *Good*

Housekeeping Editorial Bulletin called *Guide to Spare Time Earning*.

The most traditional areas in which women can earn money by their own efforts at home are crafts and domestic skills. Knitting, patchwork, soft toy making, macramé – the whole range of attractive goods that sell in craft shops and markets – are made very largely in private homes. Good cooks can earn pennies by producing cakes and bread for their local Women's Institute market – contact your local WI market to find out how to go about this. Or they can undertake private dinner parties or freezer filling. An advertisement in the local food shop or the local paper can help you to get started.

If you have extra room in your house you can consider doing bed and breakfast if you live in a tourist area, or taking in lodgers. Foreign language schools are often looking for families to take in their students, or you could try contacting the personnel or accommodations officer of any large organisation in your area if you have accommodation to let. If you are thinking of using your house in this way make sure that you know your rights under law. The Department of the Environment publishes some useful booklets to help you here. Look for *Rooms to Let, Landlords and the Law* and *Letting your own Home*. Your local Citizens Advice Bureau may have them or will tell you how to get them.

If you have land as well as room, then the least you can do is supplement the family diet and stretch the housekeeping by producing fruit and vegetables. At best you can grow a surplus which is worth selling, or you can give house room to some productive animals like chickens, goats or bees. But check your local by-laws to make sure that you are allowed to keep animals. And it is wise to warn the neighbours.

If you have a skill or some specialised knowledge, consider teaching it. Typing of a high quality can bring you a constant supply of freelance work, especially if you invest in a really good electric typewriter. If you can teach music or languages or any exam subject, advertise for pupils. If you are professionally qualified in law or translation or proof-reading or auditing, you don't need me to tell you how to go about getting clients. You might also consider basic craft skills such as electrical work or radio and television repairs which can be done at home. And if you don't have a particular skill yourself, have you thought of being a clearing house for other people?

Running an agency of this kind – whether for secretarial work, domestic cleaners, employment, publicity or literary – really comes under the heading of starting your own business. This involves other people. It involves contracts and legal agreements and tax and this is where you lift yourself out of the cottage industry into a field where you need to be both professional yourself, and professionally advised. Happily there is no shortage of excellent free advice available to anyone who is thinking of setting up business on their own. I have listed some of the sources of this advice at the end of the book.

The first thing to consider is how you want to earn your money. What is your idea? Is it a product? A brilliantly designed baby sling or a range of home-made herbal cosmetics? Is it a service – a specialised public relations agency or a personal introduction bureau? Is it a shop or a restaurant or a hotel? Or is it simply you – you and your commissioned murals for offices and shopping centres? You and your amazing hats? You and your research service for writers and journalists? Unless you are already expert in the running of shops or the writing of articles it would be a good idea to get some experience first. You might find that you are no good, or that however much the idea of running a flower shop appeals in the abstract, you are allergic to flowers and hate customers.

If you know exactly what it is you want to do and you know you can do it, can you persuade other people to pay for it? Are there half a dozen other ladies filling freezers in your small town? Can a well-known, big firm turn out children's clothes better and cheaper than you can? Or, if you specialise in intricate hand-embroidered cushion covers, will the sheer hours put in make them so expensive that nobody can afford to pay for them? The costing is the trickiest part of the whole business.

If you are convinced that there is a demand and you can supply it at a reasonable price, ask yourself a much tougher question. How much can you afford to lose? I met an antique dealer once who had just sold her vacuum cleaner. It was not an antique and valuable vacuum cleaner but she had not sold anything else that week and the rent and rates had to be paid. Look hard at the amount of expense you will be incurring and consider what capital you have to cover it until you start earning money. Work done is not money earned until your customers have paid up and the cheque is in your bank account. Working for yourself can be a very hand-to-mouth existence, even at the highest level.

You could do worse at this early stage than read a lucid and valuable little book produced by the Small Firms Information Service. It is called *Starting a Manufacturing Business* and it includes a probing little checklist entitled 'Self Appraisal – the Human Side'. '*Ask yourself,*' it says mercilessly, ' *"am I prepared to work hard and for long hours? This may mean working 70 hours a week, 50 – 52 weeks a year until the business grows to the point where you can afford to employ people. Am I prepared to give up my leisure hobbies if they interfere with the running of the business? Is my health sufficiently good to enable me to do the job and not have much sick leave?"*'

Most working mothers are going to answer 'No', to all this. They have enough on their plates as it is, so if you still want to run your own business you will have to exercise the discipline required to keep it manageable from the start. One of the biggest temptations facing the self-employed is a desperate need to take on any and every piece of work that comes their way in case they never get offered any more. Don't get caught this way. Start small. Risk no more capital than you can afford to use. Don't employ anybody until you know it will pay you to do so, until your time is more valuable than theirs. Don't invest in expensive premises or expensive stock.

Your best resources in the very beginning are your own home, some basic item of equipment like a sewing machine, a typewriter or a freezer and your own wits, talent and experience. And remember that – although you must be sure to take professional advice from your bank manager, an accountant and a solicitor before you do anything irrevocable – you cannot do anything at all without the support of your own family, in particular your husband. Running your own business can be a lonely and vulnerable way of managing a working life and you need plenty of ears to bend, shoulders to cry on and people who are prepared to put up with baked beans on those occasions when efficiency slips.

13   Mothers and Money

The richest woman in the world is a working mother. She is the Queen. Up there in her league is another working mother – ex-Queen Juliana of the Netherlands. Elizabeth Taylor can't be doing badly and even Margaret Thatcher, though a mere employee of the state, earns a well above average salary. So working mothers can be high earners if they find the right job. But unfortunately your average working mother not only earns less than men, she earns less than other women. Forget the palaces dotted about the world, the film star furs and legendary diamonds that are the perks of some working mothers' jobs. The hard facts of the matter are that the average earnings of the mothers in the *Woman's Own* survey were 90p an hour, compared with £1.48 an hour for other women and £2.49 an hour for men.

The New Earnings Survey of April 1978 found that the proportion of male manual workers with gross weekly earnings under £50 was 6.4% but the proportion of women was 57.2% and 10% of manual women workers had earnings under £34 a week. These figures reflect the fact that most working mothers are crowded into badly paid, unskilled, part-time work. Of course, if you raise your ambitions towards a career, then you can be earning money on a par with executive men, but as we have already seen, only 12% of professional workers are women. And one study of managerial women found that they were still paid on a slightly lower scale and with fewer perks than their male colleagues.

The Equal Pay Act, like the Sex Discrimination Act has been but a ripple on the surface of the problem. The failure lies in the way the Act works. Jean Coussins, in her book *The Equality Report*, published by the National Council for Civil Liberties points out that *'common sense tells her [a woman claimant] that equal pay should mean, simply, the proper rate for the job regardless of the sex of the person doing it. Yet the law tells us she has no such case unless there is actually a man doing the same work.'*

So for lack of direct comparison, many women remain on low rates of pay which simply do not apply to their male colleagues. In 1978 the *Department of Employment Gazette* reported that there are still, despite the Equal Pay Act, special women's rates of pay. The National Council for Civil Liberties has dealt with many cases where employers use this imprecision in the law to get away with blatant sexism in paying their workers. Seventy paint can fillers from the firm of Bergers reported that the firm was trying to forestall an equal pay claim by calling the women 'light paint can fillers' while the men, who were doing exactly the same job, were called 'heavy paint can fillers'. The women won their case, but in another situation prejudice won when a housemother in a school for handicapped children claimed equal pay with a housefather. Paternalistic and patronising judges decided that the case did not hold water because *'a housemother is engaged to look after younger boys and carry out domestic duties. The housefather is engaged to lead the growing boys to a better approach to life and help them in their problems. The roles are largely those of a mother and father in ordinary life. They are both important but they are different – for these reasons we find that the applicant is not engaged on like work with the man, full of admiration as we are for the work which she is doing.'* (This is a useful case to quote, incidentally, when the question of the value of motherhood comes up. Quite clearly in official eyes it is not only different from fatherhood, it is worth less.)

Part-time working is still used as a universal excuse for paying women less than men. A woman worker in a coat factory worked 27 hours a week for £1.61 an hour, whereas a man who was doing exactly the same job for forty hours a week was paid £1.67 an hour. With more unions campaigning for a shorter working week this division between part-time (at thirty hours a week and below) and full-time work (which could be a 35 hour week) is going to be more and more artificial in the future. Women can only work their way through this legislation and prejudice with the help of their trade unions. Just as with sex discrimination, the law is there and it is an imperfect law, but it must be tested and improved with more and more cases.

Whatever the working mother brings into the household, whether it is £10 a week or £100, each family works out its own way of balancing the budget and the power structure in the house. In the past it was easier to think of the woman's money as 'pin money' than it is now, but for a great many women, the idea lingers that their money ought to be for jam not bread and that the pleasure goes out of the whole business when what ought to be a night out or a new winter coat disappears into the electricity bill. That is a feeling men have always known.

In houses where the woman is the breadwinner there is none of this wishful thinking about a secondary salary. Money is for survival and that's it, and the family has to put up with the inconveniences of having a full-time working mother in order to keep their noses above the breadline. *'My son came in one day,'* said a single parent, *'and said "when are we going to get a decent meal around here?" and I said, "OK it's your choice. I can stay in the house on supplementary benefit and you can have the house cleaned and you can earn your own pocket money and go without holidays and outings or – " and they said, "OK you work." I rent a place and the rest of the money goes on food. I give the kids hand-me-downs to wear. My teenage daughter has a clothing allowance of £1 a week and I wear her hand-me-downs. The rest I pick up at Dr. Barnado's. For holidays we've stayed at a friend's caravan at Sussex and once, five years ago, I borrowed £400 and bought a VW mini bus and took the children all over the Continent. Then I sold it when we got back because I needed the money. I've got a £50 car now and I use about 3 gallons of petrol a week and I went to car maintenance classes so I could do my own repairs. When I was on supplementary benefit and I wasn't working I managed to live on it because I was at home and I could cook beans in ten different ways. Teenagers are terribly expensive. They all eat much more than I do, they grow out of their clothes and then there's always school treats. I've just had a rise and the thing that's impressed my kids most of all about my promotion is that it means they no longer qualify for free school meals. This has symbolised something important to them.'*

If a woman knows that she is going to be solely responsible for the upkeep of herself and her family it can bring about a much more hard-headed attitude to money. One mother who, up until her divorce, had always been fairly sheltered, deliberately looked, not just for a job, but for a well-paid job.

'Knowing that we were going to separate, the first thing for me to do was to find a job in which I could be independent. I had to get a job which could support me, in other words, relatively well paid. Had I gone straight into work as a secretary I would have had a very hard time. I never had alimony myself. I felt extremely insecure about the whole thing, but after I'd been working and paid for about six or seven years, I knew that I could manage.

Part of my husband's argument at the time of the break-up was that I couldn't look after myself and I wasn't sure of myself for a long time afterwards.'

This traditional attitude that the woman could never be the main breadwinner, that the woman's earning are essentially frivolous, can be very undermining to female self-confidence and contributes substantially to women's comparatively undemanding approach to pay and employers. The Secretary of State for Social Services wrote to the National Council for Civil Liberties in 1975 and articulated the official view on the matter.

'It is normal for a married woman in this country to be primarily supported by her husband and she looks to him for support when not actually working rather than to a Social Security benefit. If she works she may still require her husband's support during substantial periods of their married life. The number of instances of the wife having the chance to be the breadwinner, as opposed to having taken on that role is still very small. Indeed, it continues to be a widespread view that a husband who is capable of work has a duty to society as well as to his wife, to provide the primary support for the family.'

But primary support, in inflationary times, is no longer adequate to keep up any but the most basic standard of living, unless the husband is very well paid. The Bermondsey study into Women Working found that the women invariably worked to increase their family's standard of living. They could help towards buying a car, to pay a mortgage rather than rent, to furnish a house, to buy clothes for the children, all items that are on the border-line between luxury and necessity.

'Life is quite different if you've got a bit of money,' said one wife simply, and that applies at whatever standard you live, whether a bit of money means a country cottage or private schools for the children or simply not having to worry about the bill when you stand at the check-out counter at Tesco.

Having a bit of money is the common lot of girls before they get married these days. It can be a horrid shock to go from being a carefree spender who wanders the boutiques on a Saturday, to somebody who can only shop with a pram and has to work out how to stretch a pound of mince for two meals. It can make a woman feel very resentful of her marriage and very trapped when she has to ask her husband, however generous, to hand out money that in the past she could have spent freely on her own account. No wonder that, as any marriage guidance expert could tell you, money is the strongest wedge in changing the balance of power in the home. It brings the woman back up on to her husband's level and sometimes, if she turns out to be the most successful earner, above it.

How couples organise their finances is as personal an area of their marriage as sex. The joint account so often advised to married couples works best when only one of them is earning and the account guarantees free access to the family money for both partners. When the husband and wife are both earning, it seems to be more common for them to want to hang on to what they've got, then chip into a common pool, just as they might if they were single flat sharers.

'*Our finances are rather muddled,*' says one member of the 'jar-in-the kitchen' school of ecomomic thought. '*We don't share a bank account. If he pays the nanny, I pay for the shopping. We put money in a purse in the kitchen and the nanny tells us when it's finished. I pay the nanny £40 a week plus food and stamp. I pay for my daughter's play school – that's £300 a year, we share the mortgage and Paul pays the bills. I have a company car and the holidays we take are mixed in with business.*'

'*We pool the money and we have separate accounts,*' says another. '*I pay for the nanny, of course – £35 a week. He pays for the mortgage and we go halves on everything else.*'

'*Basically Michael is the breadwinner,*' explains a third. '*If I stopped working tomorrow it wouldn't affect the family finances. I provide the help, which is lavish – a daily nanny, a live-in housekeeper, a part-time secretary. We have a big house, much larger than we need. We get more cultural treats than most – theatres and concerts – but the children are dressed from Marks & Spencer.*'

These women are all high earners, in the over £10,000 bracket, but it is worth noting that every working mother spends the bulk of her salary on the same thing – providing a substitute for herself. This mother earns £37 a week before tax for a nine to five clerical job. '*The local registered childminder wanted to be paid 30p an hour for my two year old daughter – a total weekly outlay of £15. Taking that slice of my wages, the tax, plus a substantial weekly cost of about £7 a week for bus fares and lunches, it has absolutely killed any incentive. I was practically paying to go to work.*'

Apart from seeing your money vanish into child care and gas bills, not new clothes and make up, the most boring part of being a working wife and mother as opposed to a working girl, is the nightmare of having your finances suddenly and inextricably bound up with someone else's. Until there is any radical reform of the income tax system in Britain, a wife hardly exists as far as the Inland Revenue are concerned, except as an appendage of her husband. Unless you get to a high enough earnings level to disentangle yourself from your husband, and become independent again, you must face up to a future of second class citizenship. *'It made me very angry when we were taxed together,'* says one wife who managed to break free, and millions of women feel the same.

The Inland Revenue, once you are married, addresses all correspondence about your own tax affairs, or your joint tax affairs to your husband. Even if you write to them yourself, it will still send an answer to your husband as though you did not exist. If you are entitled to a tax rebate it will send it to your husband. The only cheering thing about it is that it will send your tax demands to him as well. Here is an outline of the income tax system as it affects married, separated, divorced and widowed women.

Normally the husband and wife are treated as one, and the husband becomes legally responsible for the couple's joint tax affairs. He is the partner who completes your tax return, claims any allowances and is automatically liable for tax due on your joint income. There are two ways of taxing married couples apart from this. One is separate assessment. The other is separate taxation of the wife's earnings or wife's earnings election, which requires the agreement of both husband and wife.

The basic system of taxing married couples requires the husband to complete one tax return which shows both his wife's and his own income. He may claim a married man's allowance which is currently £2,145 and any other allowances which are due to him or his wife including the wife's earned income allowance. All or part of these allowances may be set against the wife's earnings if the husband's income (including his and his wife's investment income) is less than the total of the allowances. He is completely responsible for payment of any tax due on his wife's unearned income – this means investment income or rent for example. His wife is allowed to claim the wife's earned income allowance against her own earnings up to a maximum limit which is the same as a single person's allowance of £1,375. This can only be set against her earned income, not against her unearned income. A wife has her own PAYE code and normally receives direct any repayments due on PAYE tax deducted from her earnings.

Repayment

The general rule is that the husband is entitled to receive any repayment of tax due since he has overall responsibility for the tax due on the couple's earnings. But the wife is entitled to her own repayment as follows:

1. Any repayment arising as a result of a change in her PAYE code due during the year.
2. Any repayment of PAYE tax due during the year because she stops work or becomes unemployed.
3. Any repayment of PAYE tax deducted from her earnings which is due at the end of the year. This does not apply if the wife has professional or business income which is not dealt with through the PAYE code, or if the couple's joint income is liable at the higher rates of tax. In addition, repayments are due direct when she and her husband claim separate investments or if the couple has elected for separate taxation of the wife's earnings.

Separate Assessment

This does not reduce the total amount of tax which the couple pays but it makes both husband and wife responsible for handling their own tax affairs and for the payment of their individual share of the tax. They may complete separate returns of their own income on separate forms. An application for separate assessment must be made in the six months before the 6th July of the tax year for which it is first to apply. To learn more about separate assessment see Leaflet IR32 *Separate Assessment*, available from your local Inland Revenue Office.

Separate Election

A couple may jointly decide to have the wife's earnings taxed separately as if she were a single person with no other income. She is then responsible for paying her own tax and she is entitled to receive any tax rebates due to her. The husband is taxed on his own earnings but he remains responsible for making a return of his wife's earnings unless application is also made for separate assessment. The wife can claim any tax relief which would be available to a single woman, such as life insurance premiums, dependent relatives allowance and so on. If the couple decide to have separate election the following apply:

1. The wife is given the single person's allowance instead of the wife's earned income allowance.

2. The husband receives a single person's allowance instead of the married man's allowance.

3. The husband continues to be responsible for tax on any investment income of his wife.

4. An election for separate taxation of the wife's earnings will not reduce the total tax bill – and could increase it – unless the couple are paying tax at the higher rate, and may not reduce it even then. Leaflet IR13 *Income Tax – Wife's Earnings Election*, explains the level of income at which an election may be to the couple's financial benefit. In the tax year 1978 – 1979, for example, it would not have been worth while for a couple to have chosen separate taxation of the wife's earnings unless their joint gross income before any deduction of personal allowances and reliefs was at least £12,449. Married couples who want a wife's earnings election must apply by:

a. giving notice of election on form 14, available from their local tax office, and

b. filling in the form and sending it to the tax office to which the husband normally makes his tax return.

Election should be made not earlier than six months before the beginning of the tax year for which you want the election to apply and not later than twelve months after the end of that tax year. It will remain in force until you give joint notice of withdrawal on form 14 – 1.

If you become separated, divorced or widowed you should inform your local tax office immediately. From the date on which you become separated, divorced or widowed you are accounted as responsible for your own tax. You can find out your tax situation in detail by reading leaflets IR30 *Separation and Divorce*, and IR23 *Income Tax and Widows*.

If you are *self-employed*, you are taxed under Schedule D and the system works differently. All the rules which apply to married couples still apply to you if you are a self-employed married woman, but the methods of calculating and paying tax are different. You can find full details of this in an Inland Revenue booklet IR28 *Starting in Business* which you can get from your local tax office.

If you are fully self-employed, or are about to become self-employed or are even self-employed in your own time, as well as doing a full-time job, inform your tax inspector. People who are taxed on Schedule D are entitled to set a number of expenses against tax and this applies, even if you have another job. What these expenses are depends largely on how you earn your living, but they include wages paid to employees (except those involved in child care) entertaining overseas customers, travel in the course of business, use of car in the course of business, VAT if you earn over £13,500 per year, legal, professional and trade union subscriptions and fees, stationery, office equipment, subscriptions to professional journals, research costs, and work materials such as paper, paint, sewing materials, potters clay, and so on. If you work at home you can deduct a proportion of the cost of running your home, although accountants advise against setting aside a special room as such because, if you come to sell your house, you may become liable for Capital Gains tax.

Let us say you work as a secretary during the day but in the evenings and at weekends you write a novel or do dress making. This extra income is taxable under Schedule D but you can set your expenses against it, even if the rest of your income is taxed under PAYE. It is quite likely that your expenses may be higher than the income you get out of your spare time earnings, but this loss could then be set against your other tax and could be an advantage to you.

It is highly advisable, if you become self-employed to whatever degree, to employ a qualified accountant to present your case to the tax inspector on your behalf and to advise you on the various expenses that you can offset against tax. No accountant should charge you more than he saves you in tax and it is well worth the reduction in ignorance and worry. And the accountant's fee counts as one of your expenses too. Self-employed people pay Class 2 National Insurance contributions which currently stand at £2.10 a week. They also pay something called Class 4 contributions which are actually another form of income tax only applicable to self-employed people. Class 4 contributions are 5% of income payable on taxable earnings between £2,000 and £6,250. A lucid account of income tax as it applies to the self-employed can be

127

found in '*The Writers' and Artists' Year Book*' in your local library, or you can find out more about it in handbooks for the self-employed, listed at the end of the book.

You will notice that working mothers are not entitled to claim the expenses of child care against their income tax. In the United States there is a $400 tax allowance for working mothers but in this country the law makes no concessions and the law has been tested to its limit. It seems particularly unjust that single mothers who *must* go to work and pay to have their children cared for get no help with this double burden. Without the child care no working mother is in any position to become part of the workforce and to contribute to the general wealth of the country. One single parent, a writer called Cathy Itzin, decided to fight this. Outraged by her accountant's suggestions that she should describe the baby-sitting costs incurred while she was theatre reviewing as 'secretarial', the standard evasion used by working mothers, she decided to claim her baby-sitting costs against tax and see what happened.

She was refused so she appealed. Each time she lost she appealed again and stopped just short of the House of Lords. What is maddening or encouraging, according to your point of view, is that the tax authorities were sympathetic to her case, but their final argument was that her baby-sitting costs were not allowable against tax as a justifiable working expense because she needed a baby-sitter because she had children, not because she was working. The expense of unravelling this piece of sophistry any further decided Cathy Itzin and her many supporters to drop the case. In the meantime Ms Itzin has tempted the tax inspectors with a new dodge. On her last income tax form she put down her baby-sitting costs, then lightly crossed through the words 'baby-sitter' and wrote 'secretary' at its side. She is waiting to see what the tax authorites will do about her blatant lie.

The point of law on which the tax inspectors based their case against Cathy Itzin was that, in order to qualify as an allowable business expense there must be no 'duality of purpose'. For example, a tax payer who claimed his lunches eaten away from home was refused. It was decided that he ate lunch in order to stay alive, not in order to work. A duality of purpose was decided to exist in the Cathy Itzin case too. There is nothing illegal, however, in claiming a portion of your nanny's wages for that work which is related to yours – for answering the telephone, for example, or delivering work for you. This can hardly apply, of course, to the childminder or the nursery so richer mummies win out again. If you want to know more about the income tax laws as they affect working mothers, then I suggest you read *Income Tax and Sex Discrimination* by Patricia Hewitt, published by the National Council for Civil Liberties.

Part Four
Working Mothers and Trouble

14   One Parent Families

One parent families may be surprised to see themselves squeezed into so small a space in this book. This is because most of the rest of the book applies to them too. What I have tried to do in this chapter is direct some extra attention to some areas which are *only* applicable to one parent families, and to point to some places where they are likely to get especially sympathetic and knowledgeable help. There is no doubt that they need it. Over half the people receiving Family Income Supplement are single parents and most of these are single mothers. The income of the average one parent family is about half that of the normal two parent family but the cost of living remains the same. One in six one parent families depends completely on the state for support compared with one in 500 two parent families. And 77% of children from one parent families claim free school meals compared with only 8% of children with two parents.

The number of one parent families grows every day. One in nine families is a one parent family and that includes one and a half million children. The worst of being a one parent family, apart from the constant effort to avoid the gaping poverty trap, is the lack of protection and choice. Single parents have to work or they end up claiming supplementary benefit. They have twice the strain of parenthood and half the help. The help there is, is meagre and grudgingly given, and in addition to the solitary financial burden of raising a family single-handed, the lone parent has nobody with whom to share the emotional and mental stresses (and pleasures) of family life. Work may be a necessity, not just because of the money, but because it is the only way that single parents can provide themselves with social life and a taste, however small, of the full flavour of the adult world.

It is easy for me to say that lone working mothers need not feel guilt about working and leaving their children because their work is a matter of survival, not personal whim. But the fact is that many lone mothers *do* feel guilt. They feel guilt because they think their mismanagement of their own lives has somehow got themselves and their children into this hopeless mess. They feel guilt because they may have to assemble a rickety structure of child care to cope with their many absences. They feel guilt because the never-ending strain of making ends meet, of coping with the relentless demands of a job and a family, of dealing with their own loneliness and the remnants of the relationship with the children's father can often lead to them placing a double burden on their children's heads.

The children suffer the normal practical problems of having a working mother and the emotional strain of having a mother so exhausted and pressured that even when she is with them she may only snap and snarl. The more the tension mounts, the more stressful the mother can find the double act of work and motherhood. Single mothers are also haunted by the prospect of what might happen to their children if they lose their jobs or if they become ill from worry and exhaustion. Whatever the problems of working and bringing up children simultaneously, lone parents have them to an infinitely greater extent than mothers who can rely on the support of a husband, which is why, although many of the problems are dealt with elsewhere, I wanted this separate chapter to concentrate on them as they affect lone parents.

Two principal organisations exist in order to guide lone parents through the mine-fields ahead of them. They are both invaluable sources of information on your rights and on assistance which may be available to you, and one, Gingerbread, offers plenty of moral support through its local lone parent self-help groups. The National Council for One Parent Families is a body which grew up from the old voluntary organisation for the unmarried mother and her child, and has since widened its scope to take in all lone parents. It acts as an information centre and pressure group for lone parents and keeps a register of family holiday swops. Gingerbread is a self-help organisation which was started by a single mother with two children and is run, countrywide, by and for lone parents and their children. Local Gingerbread groups run a variety of services from fully fledged day care centres and holiday schemes to baby-sitting rotas and toy pools. Both organisations produce a valuable and informative list of publications on every aspect of lone parenthood from day care to tax laws and coping with social security.

A third organisation, Single Handed Limited, acts as an agency for one parent families who want to share homes and holidays, or for lone fathers and their children who would like a paid substitute mother and for single mothers and their children who are prepared to look after the lone fathers in exchange for a home and a wage. It also runs a holiday home for unaccompanied children whose desperate parents need a break, and acts as an introduction agency for one parent families to get to know each other.

However, even if you become the life and soul of your local Gingerbread group or have the luck to be in the care of a sympathetic and efficient social worker, the facts of life for most lone parents are that, when the chips are down, they must learn to be their own best support system. Lone mothers are without that basic security system which most other working mothers have to some degree – a husband. They must unlearn habits of dependence which may have taken a life time to absorb. They must learn that if they want anything at all, from new friends to a holiday to a loaf of bread from the shop, they, and nobody else, will have to go and get it. They have to learn the hard way to go it alone.

'*In a two parent family,*' says Julie Kaufmann, Director of Gingerbread, '*you've either got free child care and support or you've got another wage earner. Single parents have to do two jobs. I am nearly 40 now and my children have just come off free school meals. You just have not got the extra to give. Socially I don't find it a problem, though others do. But it's lonely when you can't say your son scored two goals in the match today – there's a limit to how interested friends are in the day-to-day development of your children.*'

Julie Kaufmann has concentrated on building up her own outside support system which can replace, to some extent, the internal one which most marriages automatically provide. '*That's why lone parents should stay in the same place,*' she says, '*to build up the support system. I know two other lone parent mums and we've known each other about 13 years and we rely heavily on each other. When I was in hospital for two weeks my neighbour came and lived in my house. I have cultivated friendships with other mothers. I'm always taking an extra child out. You can then feel alright saying "can you do this for me?"*'

A supporting community can relieve personal loneliness, provide emergency help and child care for your children and help to make up the gaps in their emotional and social experience. You cannot do everything for your children all by yourself. Resist the temptation to flee to an isolated cottage on a hillside however much you long to break away from familiar and unhappy surroundings. There is a lot to be said for staying in the place where you and your children have friends, whether it is an urban neighbourhood which offers the range of entertainments and services and life lines that you and your children need, or a suburb or village where a web of friends and neighbours can replace the range of facilities available in the big town.

If they can build up their support network at home, lone mothers also have to learn to take themselves more seriously at work. It is a bitter fact to come to terms with, but many lone mothers are the chief breadwinner for their children and are likely to be so until their children leave home. The days when the wife's income provided the gilt on the gingerbread are over. It is quite likely that her income suddenly has to provide everything and her job is no longer an indulgence but a life line. In order to provide an adequate income she may suddenly need to think about pushing herself up the job ladder, either by retraining or by applying for promotion at work.

Adopt the attitude of the mother who said, '*The first thing for me to do was to find a job in which I could be independent, a job which could support me, something relatively well paid.*' And when you have found your job, cultivate a 'masculine' attitude to work which one writer described as '*aggressive, competitive, ungrateful*'. Lone parenthood has this advantage, that divorced and separated women do not have to carry a failing marriage as well as a job. It can be easier to forge ahead at work with the incentive of caring for your children once your emotional energies are not being consumed in quarrels and unhappiness. And work is the best of all healers for emotional problems. Single parents can afford to be single-minded.

Once you have a job, I suggest you do two things. One is to take out life insurance and loss of earnings insurance, just as a man would. Your insurance broker or bank manager will advise you. Now that the breadwinner is you, your family needs extra protection should anything happen to you. And you should also inform your tax office of your single status. The Inland Revenue publish a useful leaflet called *Income Tax and One Parent Families* (IR29) which you can get at your local tax office. Lone parents are entitled to claim an income tax allowance called the additional personal allowance which, together with your single person's allowance, raises your tax allowance to the level of that of a married man. You may also be entitled to child benefit increase, so collect leaflet CBll from your local social security office. For more detailed information and advice on one parent families see the list at the end of this book.

15 Crisis

Although lone parents live nearer the danger line than most, many working mothers are beset with the anxiety that anything could snap at any moment. Sometimes it does. Disaster can strike from several different directions. You could lose your job. You could lose your husband. Your children could fall ill or the school could go on strike. Your child care arrangements could break down. You could break down. If any of these eventualities should come to pass even the most competent mother is facing a crisis and the most needy mother is facing absolute disaster. The most moving letter among all those sent in by *Woman's Own* readers came from a mother who lived through such a crisis and bears the scars to this day. I would like to quote it in full because although it tells of an extreme case, every working mother will understand what the writer went through. It underlines everything that is wrong with the help given to working mothers.

'*It was two years ago when my children were seven and four. I left my husband to go into the battered wives home in 1976, well I got my divorce and I was living on social security. I myself don't and did not like living off the government so I decided to look for work in the hours my children were at school. I got a job but it meant my children had to come home from school on their own. I arrived home about ten minutes late. Now at the time I was so confident that my children were alright but on part-time I wasn't earning enough to keep us in bread all week so I started full-time work which meant my girls had to have an alarm clock set for each morning so that they could go to school on time. I left at 7.30 a.m. and my eldest had to have a key to let them in at night, I arrived two hours later.*'

'*Now at the time I did worry. I wasn't heartless but everything seemed to be fine then came the summer holidays and to this day I can still cry for what I did. This is one thing I can never make up to my children and I can't really explain on paper what heartbreak it was for me and my children. I left them on their own all day. Oh yes they had drinks and I left sandwiches for them, they had enough to eat and drink and they could go into the back garden. But by the*' *second week I had worried myself into keep taking time off, I knew it was wrong to leave them but at the same time I couldn't go back on social security so I went to Social Services for help.*

'They said the only thing they could do was have a woman pop round at dinner time to make sure that everything was alright but by this time my nerves were so bad at the thought of leaving them alone again that I was being physically sick. I went to the personnel officer at work and explained my problems. He was very nice and tried to help. He realised that I didn't want to leave my children but at the same time I couldn't go back on social security. So he suggested going back on part-time for the time being at least it would get me home early. So I did that, also just around this time I heard of a lady who would have my children for £10 a week (I tried advertising in the paper but to no success). So I went to see her and she said she would look after them, the only thing was that being on part-time work and paying her I fell behind with my rent. In the end my nerves got so bad my children ended up in care for a month. I stopped work and went back on social security.

'I got my children back and everything went back to normal. I say that, but to this day I have nightmares of what might have happened. I have to live with guilt for the rest of my life. Even telling you doesn't help and even as I am writing this I am shaking and as you can see I find it difficult to write. If only someone could have helped me to find some way of looking after my children everything would have been fine. As it is my heart still cries for how I left my children at four years and seven years to look after themselves. In my way I was trying to help us get a better way of living. If there was some way I could go to work and knew my children were well looked after I would but until that day comes my children will never be latch key kids again. It's about time something was done to help mothers go out to work and not have small children worrying and waiting for mummy to come home. My story is just one. I wonder how many more mothers went through and are still going through what I did.'

Happily for most of us this accumulation of disaster and guilt is relatively rare, although for lone mothers it must threaten like a perpetual dark cloud in the corner of their lives. The saddest aspect of this story is that the writer, like most working mothers, was trying to do her best by everybody. But she failed to the extent of leaving her job and having her children taken into care and this is a *memento mori* for the rest of us. The fact that lone mothers think they can manage the whole working family business single-handed and cannot is a prime cause of children being taken into care.

Every working mother knows the most vulnerable point in her arrangements. Some describe diagnosing their children's illnesses over the telephone. Others leave an elaborate list of emergency numbers and addresses with their children's nurseries or baby-sitters. The better off rely on paid agency help to see them through a tight spot, although this is by no means the perfect solution. Children do not always take well to complete strangers suddenly coming to the home, especially when the atmosphere is already fraught. Those worse off have to rely on family and neighbours and the inadequate resources of the welfare state. Some are so traumatised by the experience, like the one just quoted, that they give up work until the signs are right for them to try again.

Help for the working mother in a crisis falls into two main categories, the kind you pay for and the kind you don't. If you can afford to pay for help to bridge the gap in the case of stricken nannies, nursery on strike, or your own illness, the agencies I list at the end of the book are geared up to provide emergency baby-sitters and mother substitutes – at a price. A typical range of fees from one agency prices general emergency help at from £40 a week living-in; an emergency mother to take over if you go into hospital will cost over £40 per week plus bed and board. A cook/housekeeper will cost the same, and these are basic rates. There is also an agency fee which could come to at least £10 a week.

If you cannot afford to pay for help then you can, in a desperate emergency, ask that your child be taken into care by the local council under section 1 of the Children's Act 1948. Your child may be fostered for a period of up to six months with any one family, during which time you are at liberty to take him out of care as soon as you have sorted out your particular crisis. After this six months' time limit you must give 28 days' notice. If, after a minimum period of three years in care, it still looks as though you will not be able to take him back, the local authority may assume responsibility for him. If your child is taken into care and you want him back, it is vital to keep in touch, not just because your child needs you but because it is important that the local authority knows you feel responsible for him. While your child is in care you are still liable to contribute to his support.

The other circumstances in which your child may be taken into care are if the council thinks you have abandoned him or are incapable of looking after him properly. If you find yourself in such a situation and you want to fight the decision, then you must write to the Social Services Department and object. You may have to go to court to win your child back. Your local Citizens Advice Bureau will help you in this case.

There is one other kind of crisis which can affect working mothers and their children and that is the violence you may inflict on your baby or young child under the extreme stress of overwork, financial insecurity and the depression that follows childbirth. There is no proof that working mothers are any more likely to batter their children than non-working mothers – in fact the break from home and children that a job provides can be a great help in relieving family tension. But mothers of babies who have to go out to work can become very overwrought as they struggle with yet another sleepless night, knowing that they have to get up in the morning and cope with a job on top of an exhausting child.

If you find yourself becoming hysterical and overwrought with your children, and especially if you feel violent towards the baby, there are a growing number of sources of help for you. These feelings of violence towards children may be a cause for fear, but they need not be a cause for guilt. So many parents have been through them that the National Children's Centre publishes a list of over 39 parents' Help Lines run along the anonymous lines of the Samaritans. They are staffed by parents and people trained in child welfare and counselling, and they exist to provide an outlet for other desperate parents. Nobody will be shocked if you ring up and say you are on the point of beating your child's brains out because the volunteers who run these groups have been through this situation themselves. All of these groups will provide a sympathetic ear. Some will be able to give more concrete assistance. If you cannot find the number of one of these groups in your area, ring the local branch of the *NSPCC* or the Samaritans. They will either be able to give you such a number or be able to help you themselves. I include a list of these groups as compiled by the National Children's Centre at the end of the book.

16   Parents and Social Security

As a last resort parents in difficulties can seek help from the state. Many families are dependent on it to a greater or lesser extent, but I have not come across a single parent who did not hate every minute of this dependence, who did not run the most awful risks of health and sanity to free herself from it. Julie Kaufmann of Gingerbread recalls her days on supplementary benefit with horror. '*I was on it for nine months and I loathed and detested it. People from social security would come and see me, usually men, and made it clear that they objected to giving me anything. One looked out of my window over towards the slums, and he said, "There are places for people like you down there."*'

Another mother had a job but she was forced to give it up for lack of child care and found herself dependent on social security. '*I wanted a nursery place, otherwise I would have to give up my job which seems silly as I was earning my own money and keeping us both and if I didn't work I would have to go on social security. The social worker said unmarried mothers and problems came first. He said I seemed able to keep my head so they just left it at that. So I had to give my job up and go on social security for a few months which I can tell you was just terrible, I felt like an outcast. They made you feel like a sponger and I only got £4 from them anyway.*'

Diana Davenport, the author of a useful and cheering book called *One Parent Families* has some cynical and practical advice for a woman unfortunate enough to be dependent on the state for assistance. '*When a social security man calls,*' she says, '*do not clean up, wash up, change into your latest hand-me-downs, wipe the children's faces, or attempt to stop the baby from indulging in his usual afternoon yell. Do not, in short, do anything which might suggest to the visitor that you can cope.*'

Many lone mothers and others have learnt the bitter truth of this piece of pragmatism in their search for help from the state in all its guises. Whereas voluntary organisations may start off on the parent's side and treat the people who seek their help as human beings, there seems to be something about government welfare which breeds suspicion in its workers and leads them to see scroungers in every corner. The strongest complaint is that the helping hand of the welfare state is not extended until a family is well and truly in the gutter. The help – particularly with child care – which might keep a family together, never seems to be there when it is most needed. Before a cheque will be issued the family morale must take yet more blows from officialdom.

'*I had been bringing my children up alone for four years,*' wrote a *Woman's Own* reader. '*I have longed to go out to work for some considerable time and have discovered lots of factors which make this extremely difficult. In one particular incidence, when I went to a council day nursery trying to enrol my son, I was told that they supported and helped those who found it difficult to manage and that they thought I was a very capable person and not needing help. So I live on maintenance payments and child benefit with help with rent and rates rebate. This has been my source of income for the last two years. Previous to this I had supplementary benefit. If I was given help in minding the children I would not be called a parasite on society or my ex-husband.*'

God, it seems, helps those who help themselves, but the state does not. Being given help too late can be almost worse than no help at all. A nursery place in time means a working mother and a self-supporting and – equally important – a self-respecting family, rather than a willing to work mother queuing miserably in the social security office and, at worst, children separated from their mother and taken into care because the strain of the whole juggling act has proved too much for her. In the profound hope that you and your family never face this problem, I have outlined the social security system as it affects parents. Nearly everybody except those claiming social security benefits, is obliged to pay a National Insurance stamp to the government. Until May 1977 married women had a choice about whether they paid National Insurance contributions. They could either pay full contributions as single women did, or they could pay reduced contributions or they could opt out and rely on their husband's National Insurance. This does not apply any longer. If you had opted out of the system before May 1977 you can choose to opt back in, but you can no longer choose to opt out.

There are three different classes of contribution. Class I is the stamp paid by everybody who works and pays tax under PAYE. Class 2 is the self-employed person's rate which is currently £2.10

a week for both men and women. And Class 3 is a reduced contribution. Class 4 is not exactly an insurance stamp, but a special tax levied on the self-employed which I explained on page 127.

In return for these weekly payments you are entitled to certain benefits. People often talk about a National Insurance stamp as the National Health stamp, but in fact only 8% of it goes to the National Health Service. The rest goes on providing the wide range of unemployment, sickness, old age, child and supplementary benefits available under the welfare state. Certain of these are of special interest to parents, working or otherwise.

The first of these is unemployment benefit. If you pay Class 2 contributions you are not eligible to collect unemployment benefit. If you are entitled to collect it, you should go to your local Employment Exchange or Job Centre as soon as you are out of work, taking with you your form P45, the income tax form which should have been given to you by your ex-employer. If you do not have a P45, tell them your National Insurance number and if you do not know your National Insurance number, go first to your local social security office and find out before you present yourself at the employment exchange.

At the employment exchange you must sign on as being available for work and therefore entitled to collect unemployment benefit. The Posy Simmonds cartoon in *Women's Rights* by Anna Coote and Tess Gill, shows a lady sporting a badge with the letters DHSS. '*It stands for "Desperate Hours of Sitting and Self Control"*,' she says cheerfully which just about sums it up. You may not get any money at all for several weeks because they have to check up on your records first. In any case, you will get no benefit for the first three days on which you were unemployed, or for time on holiday, or time spent abroad, or if they decide you are turning down work, or if you are awarded a sum by an industrial tribunal under the provisions of the Employment Protection Act. You stop getting unemployment benefit after you have been claiming it for a year.

The information I give you here is very simplified. If you find yourself unemployed I strongly recommend that you read a good handbook explaining your rights, such as *Women's Rights* by Anna Coote and Tess Gill, and that you go to your local Department of

Health and Social Security office or Citizens Advice Bureau and ask somebody to explain to you what you should do.

You may also be entitled to *sickness benefit* if you fall ill while working. You can find a full explanation of sickness benefit in National Insurance leaflet NI16, available from your local social security office. It is payable for a maximum period of 28 weeks to a claimant who is incapable of work due to sickness or disablement, if the relevant National Insurance contributions have been made. Only employed persons who pay Class 1 contributions or self-employed persons who pay Class 2 contributions qualify for sickness benefit. It is £18.50 a week for each claimant plus £11.45 for each dependent adult, and £1.70 for each dependent child. It is not payable for the first three days on which you are ill and not working. Earnings-related supplement is also payable up to a maximum supplement of £17.67 a week for a maximum period of 26 weeks beginning after the twelfth consecutive day in any period of unemployment.

Family Income Supplement is a benefit that you can claim if you simply cannot earn enough to live on, and the authorities agree with you. You can read more about it in leaflet FIS 1, available from your local social security office. The head of the household must be in full-time work, there must be at least one dependent child in the family, and the family's normal gross weekly income must be below a prescribed level. A claim can be made by a lone parent and by the self-employed. Full-time work is defined as thirty hours or more a week, and in the case of a couple, the head of the household is defined as a man. The level of income below which the Family Income Supplement can be received depends on the number of children in the family. When calculating the level of income, the following do not count as income: child benefit, the first £4 of a war disablement pension, children's income, the whole of any attendance and mobility allowance and rent allowances.

The prescribed weekly amount for any family from January 1980 is £56 for a family with one child plus £4.50 for each additional child. The weekly rate of a Family Income Supplement will be half of the amount by which the family income falls short of the prescribed amount. The maximum payment is £13.50 for families with one child, increasing by £1 for each additional child. The award is usually made for 52 weeks and the rate of payment is not affected by any change in circumstance, whether favourable

145

or not. People who receive Family Income Supplement are also entitled to free NHS prescriptions, dental treatment and spectacles, free milk and vitamins for expectant mothers and children under school age, free school meals, refund of fares to hospital and free legal advice and assistance. It is worth pointing out that the legislation for Family Income Supplement does not recognise the woman as head of the household even though she may be the breadwinner and even though the husband may be incapable of work.

The other benefits which affect working parents are *child benefit* which is payable for all children who are either under 16, or under 19 and still in full-time education. The rate is £4.75 per week per child from November 1980. An extra benefit of £3 per week is payable for the first or only child in a one parent family. If you want to know how to claim child benefit, get form CB 1 from your local social security office. You will also find leaflet FB1 *Family Benefits and Pensions* useful.

Supplementary benefit is the safety net that one parent families dread. It is a non-contributory benefit – it means that you are entitled to it whether you pay National Insurance contributions or not – which can be paid to anyone aged 16 or over who has left school and is not in full-time work. The amount of benefit paid is the difference between a person's resources and his requirements under the scheme. Resources are defined as:

1. earnings – in the case of single parents £6 of earnings is ignored before earnings are taken into account;

2. child benefit and most National Insurance benefits and maintenance payments;

3. any other weekly income excluding the first £4.

Your requirements are then made up from the appropriate scale rates plus some addition for rent and any special additions to which the claimant is entitled. The householder will usually have his rent and rates allowed in full, and other outgoings such as mortgage interest are allowable. The benefits range from a maximum of £29.70 for a married couple to £5.20 for children under five. To find out more about supplementary benefit, read leaflets FB 1, SB 2 and SB 9 from your local social security office. If you are very hard up you may also be entitled to rent or rate rebates. Check with your Citizens Advice Bureau and ask for their leaflets *How to Pay Less Rates* and *There's Money Off Rent*.

Part Five
Conclusion

17   Working Together

The essence of the problem for the working mother is that she still bears the greatest burden of responsibility for the family and the day-to-day care of her children. The mother is where the buck stops. The fact that more and more mothers are taking on a full-time responsibility outside the home has done little, so far, to change the balance either way. When the crunch comes it is the mother who looks after the children when they are ill, the mother who remembers to buy them new shoes and lay in the fish fingers, the mother who has to find and pay for the nursery place or the nanny, and the mother who must make time to campaign for a crèche at work.

However liberated the wife, however sharing and caring the husband, however permissively brought up the children, the family still unite, often unconsciously, to reinforce the mother's primary position. Children who wake in the night call out for mummy, even if she has to be up three hours later to catch the 8.45. *'In the end,'* reports one working mother who goes out to the office all day while her husband works at home, *'I probably have prime responsibility for the children, and I think the children assume that I have prime responsibility, which is interesting. I am elected to decide even about trivial things and if they want to go out then I have to give permission.'*

It is no wonder that mothers start off with a different attitude to paid work from their husbands. Men may be taking on more family duties through force of circumstance, but most of them have been brought up from birth *not* to think about this family responsibility except as breadwinners. Success for men means working competitively and getting to the top in their chosen career. Success for women means getting the balance of their lives right.

'I learned,' wrote Mary Kenny, *'that women are scarcely ever ambitious in the sense of wanting to get to the very top because most women consider the price too high. Women are often less obsessive about their work but more serious about it. Women are forced to think of work in terms of priorities.'*

Success for the working mother is entirely dependent on the help she gets. In Bermondsey, the research workers found that there were very few problems for working mothers and their families because *'there was lots of part time work, a wide variety of working hours, good leisure provisions for children. The inter-related stable history of the population eased the practical problems and lessened the physical dangers. The long tradition of the mother going out to work meant that the technique of coping with a dual job had been tested by that time. So many Bermondsey children have a mother who works that it is the norm. When the wives took the evening shift it was the husband who regularly took the care of the children.'*

In their book, *Fathers, Mothers and Others*, the sociologists Rhona and Robert Rapoport and their colleagues discovered that *'the most successful pattern of child rearing appeared to be the "co-ordinate marriage". A study showed that good management and high income eased the burden of integrating family and work. It works better when a wife alone is not responsible for the care of the house and children and it involves proper co-ordination, not role reversal. The happiness of a co-ordinate marriage increases when the husband's work satisfaction increases and more money comes in.'*

It should not really need teams of sociologists and PhD students to come to these blindingly obvious conclusions. The answer is simplicity itself. Working mothers and their families thrive best when work is flexible, when children are well cared for, when husbands are sharing and when there is enough money coming into the house. The difficulties lie in scraping all these ingredients together. Somehow, outside close-knit communities like Bermondsey, the elements of success are harder to find.

In an attempt to find alternative solutions, two other ideas are often suggested. One is that where the wife is successful the answer may be for the husband to stay at home and look after the children in her place. The other is that a woman's need to work outside the home would be greatly reduced if the state payed her a sensible allowance while her children were small. Complete role reversal is only a practical possibility for the very few and its drawbacks are exactly the same as the drawbacks of more conventional arrangements. Husbands who stay at home to look after their children – even on a shift system with their wives – suffer all the isolation and frustration that their wives suffered before them, with added problems caused by being a man in a woman's world. Husbands who tried it report that other mums don't chat to them in the park, that nobody asks them round for coffee and that children in the playgroup tell them nastily that *their* daddies work. The responsibilities of parenthood are not shared in this way, but simply off-loaded on to the other partner. However, it is worth noting that it can be to a couple's financial advantage for the woman to work and the husband to stay at home as the two sets of tax allowances can be set against the single income.

I personally do not think that a motherhood allowance is a complete answer either, although some countries operate one with reasonable success. In Hungary women are paid to stay at home for the first year of their child's life with a guarantee of their job back at the end of the period. In the German Democratic Republic mother allowances are linked to the availability of day care. If a nursery place is unavailable, mothers are paid a flat grant equal to about 40% of the average wage until one falls vacant and they can return to work. The Council of Europe's Committee of Experts on Social Security have a standing recommendation that mothers with young children should receive a state allowance if they stay at home, but although a great many family budgets would be helped this way, and although it would ease the problem of enforced absence from work, it would not be the answer to all the complex reasons why women go out to work. A state grant does not provide as much money as many women could earn. It does not provide companionship or stimulation or an entrée into the outside world. Nor does it make any use of the working skills of the women it would pay to stay at home.

If the lot of working mothers and their families is to improve at all, the changes must come from husbands, employers and child care. I have dealt with child care and with women's employers in earlier chapters. It is time to acknowledge the crucial role of the husband. Few working mothers can get anywhere without one. The statistics of lone parents are evidence of the weight of the unsupported load of a family. Unfortunately no statistics exist on the problems faced by working women whose husbands are present in body but not in spirit.

When the mother goes out to work, a marriage guidance counsellor told me, it makes good marriages and it breaks bad ones. The essence of a good marriage for a working mother is to have a sensitive husband who does not take her presence and her contribution to the family for granted. Even the most loving and

151

helpful husbands have some weaknesses. How many husbands ask their wives if they will baby-sit while they go to a meeting or darts match? Precious few. If women want to go out of the house they have to make a formal arrangement, either with a baby-sitter or with their husbands. If men want to go out, they go out, with the blithe assumption that their children and the house are automatically taken care of. According to the *Woman's Own* survey, one in six husbands has never looked after his children on his own and one quarter have never put their own children to bed. The wives of husbands like these have a hard row to hoe.

The peripheral role of fathers in their children's upbringing is as much a matter of tradition and *their* upbringing as of personal choice. Like so many other things in life, it just grows, and it grows hand in hand with the idea that the mother is the person who must bear sole responsibility for her young children. Attitudes are shifting, but decades – even centuries – of the father as distant provider and occasional patter on head of infant are not going to be erased over night.

Both parents are victims of recently prevailing concepts of parenthood which, according to a survey of modern child care literature quoted by both Rapoports goes something like this. *'One, children are the most valuable resource we have, therefore children's needs should always take precedence. Two, the first few years of life are crucial and parents are responsible for this. Three, the essence of early experience is mothering. Good mothering requires constant presence of a mother. Four, the mother/child bond is biological. Five, mothers' and infants' needs are complementary. Six, father isn't directly important, except as protector and provider. Seven, parenting involves sacrifice, but the rewards balance the sacrifices and anyway, no sacrifice is too great when it comes to children, because having children brings its own rewards. People who don't accept this shouldn't have children.'*

If this is the prevailing view of parenthood, and of the mother's and father's separate roles in it, then it offers very little comfort to the millions of couples who have to work and bring their children up together. No wonder the state and the commercial world together can afford to be so unbending when it comes to helping working families do their best by work and children. They are supported by a great body of tacit disapproval of couples who try to have their cake and eat it.

Happily for the future of the family in a working world, a great many husbands are willing to play more part in their children's upbringing, not just because their wife's work forces them into it, but because they are discovering for themselves that children are a lot of fun, and they are beginning to resent the organisation of a society that excludes them from their own family.

The growing practice of allowing fathers to be present at the birth of their children must have an influence on the father's greater desire for involvement in the care of the children. How can they feel distant from and uninvolved in the new life which they saw beginning? And once fathers begin to play a larger part in their children's lives, they are often unwilling to give up this rich source of reward and pleasure. Fathers who work at home report a closer relationship with their children as one of the great bonuses of their life. They understand their own children better, and they appreciate the delight of seeing the world afresh through a child's eyes. Just as the burden of responsibility for children is too great to be borne alone, so the rewards of children are too great to be enjoyed alone.

The fly in the ointment is that most fathers at work have time-consuming, inflexible jobs. There is some acknowledgement among employers and politicians of the mother's need for maternity leave, although birth seems to be the only family event worth official recognition and paid leave. But at present, very few employers recognise the father's need for leave to help his wife over this particular hurdle or to share the work with her during other family crises such as children's illness.

Abroad, of course, the situation is different. The country which has gone furthest in reconciling family and the needs of the working world is , inevitably, Sweden, although French fathers are also allowed the option of unpaid parental leave for a period of up to two years. After this period, the father or mother is guaranteed his or her job back, as long as they have worked at least a year for their employer (who must employ at least 200 staff) and have given prior notice of their intention to take leave and return.

In Sweden the aim seems to be to remove all prejudice and difficulty from the need for parental leave so that employers will be no more upset by a request for paternal leave than they would be if one of their employees had to do national service. All parents – and that includes biological parents, adopted parents, foster parents, ex-husbands and ex-wives and unmarried parents –

are entitled to child care leave. Mothers alone are allowed 49 days over the confinement period, paid at 90% of their normal earned income. Then the parents are entitled to 210 paid days of parental leave between them. Parents whose child is under 18 months can take unlimited, unpaid parental leave, and parents with children under eight years are allowed a reduced six hour day on reduced pay. Parents with children under 10 years are allowed a quota of extra days off a year, paid at sickness benefit rates.

One example of the way this system might work in a particular family is if a mother took four months of full-time leave while she had the baby. Her husband might then take two months of full-time leave to stay home with her or replace her, and the couple could then take it in turns to work either half-time or three-quarter time up until the child's first birthday. Parents and children would, in this way, get to know each other intimately, without jobs or family life or bank balance suffering unduly. So far about 6,000 fathers of new-born babies have taken advantage of the system to stay home with their young children. The percentage is apparently small but the essence of the legislation is that the opportunity is there and that there is no stigma attached to any man or woman who takes advantage of it.

The Swedes may have pioneered this approach, but the rest of Europe is willing, in principle, to follow them. The 1975 Council of Europe Conference of Ministers Responsible for Family Affairs called on governments to support the 'symmetrical' family. For 'symmetrical' read 'balanced'. The balanced family is headed by parents who share the rights and duties of parenthood supported by increased state benefits to families with small children, and adequate parental leave and good child care facilities. The Ministers' Conference decided that by giving working parents a realistic choice between home and work and the means to divide their lives in a satisfactory way between the two, they would support, rather than divide the family. In order to help families in this way, they recommended more free or subsidised nursery care to make the parents' freedom of choice real, not theoretical.

Britain lags far behind in this new, more open-minded attitude to the family. The TUC is more progressive than Parliament in its recommendation. It has recorded its resolution that 'Equality between men and women cannot be achieved until the work of child care is both more evenly distributed between the sexes and better provided for through *parental leave and crèche facilities. To this end Conference recommends that the maternity leave provisions of the Employment Protection Act be extended to provide 12 weeks paid leave instead of 6, the extra entitlement to be take by the mother or by the father of the baby as they prefer – the aim is to establish the principle of maternity leave in law and to involve the father in the care of the baby from the beginning.'*

The aim of all the proposed legislation is a very healthy one. It is not simply to allow more mothers to dump their children and skip off to work. It is to give more protection, status and encouragement to the family as a whole. *'It will be a great day,'* says Doctor Spock, *'when fathers consider the care of their children to be as important to them as their jobs and careers, when they seek out jobs and work schedules that allow them ample time to be with their wives and children, when they give first consideration, when discussing with their wives where to live, to what favours family life, will resist their company's attempts to move them frequently, and will let it be known at their work places that they take their parental responsibilities very seriously and they have to have time off when their children need them – just as working mothers have always done, and will try to get other fathers at their work places to take the same stand.'*

Only when the whole family balances its needs together will the lives of working fathers be enriched and made more human, the lives of working mothers made easier and the lives of their children made more secure. More nurseries are not the answer on their own. Neither is flexitime or maternity leave or equal pay. But together they would help to create a climate in which life could be an adventure and each member of the family would be free to take part in it. I like the way in which this *Woman's Own* reader put it, looking back over a life of working motherhood.

'There is quite a lot needs to be done in regards to clinics, nurseries for schools, places for mothers to leave toddlers in safety even on payment. The money would be well spent and mothers would gain by not having all that worry. Again I think there should be preparation for parenthood for fathers as well as mothers. Instead of so much sex, more talk of where money is needed in the home and of respect for each other.'

Notes and References:
Useful Publications and Addresses

PUBLICATIONS OF GENERAL INTEREST

Double Shift. Barbara Toner. Arrow. 1975.

Woman × Two. Mary Kenny. Hamlyn paperbacks. 1978.

Women's Rights. Anna Coote and Tess Gill. Penguin. 1977.

But what About the Children? Judith Hann. Sphere. 1977.

Mothers – their power and influence. Ann Daly. Weidenfeld and Nicolson. 1976.

Working Mothers and Their Children. Simon Yudkin and Anthea Holme. Michael Joseph. 1963.

Married Women Working (Bermondsey Study). Pearl Jephcott, Nancy Seear, John H. Smith. Allen and Unwin. 1962.

Britain's Married Women Workers. Viola Klein. Routledge and Kegan Paul. 1965.

Women in Top Jobs. Michael Fogerty, A. J. Allen, Isobel Allen, Patricia Halters. Allen and Unwin. 1971.

Dual Career Families, 1977 and *Dual Career Families Re-Examined*. Rhona and Robert Rapoport. Martin Robertson. 1976.

Fathers, Mothers and Others. Rhona and Robert Rapoport *et al*. Routledge and Kegan Paul. 1977.

Nurseries Now. Martin Hughes, Berry Mayall, Peter Moss, Jane Perry, Pat Petrie, Gill Pinkerton, Penguin. 1980.

USEFUL PUBLICATIONS AND ADDRESSES OF SPECIFIC INTEREST

3. Good Mothers, Bad Mothers and the Rest of Us

Child Care and the Growth of Love. John Bowlby. Penguin. 1953.

The Future of Motherhood. Jessue Bernard. Dial (USA). 1974.

The Needs of Children. Mia Kellmer Pringle. Hutchinson. 1974.

4. Guilt and How to Live With It

Maternal Deprivation Re-assessed. Michael Rutter. Penguin. 1972.

Social Science and Social Pathology. Barbara Wootton. Allen and Unwin. 1959.
Book of Babycare. Miriam Stoppard. Weidenfeld and Nicolson. 1977.

5. Getting a Quart into a Pint Pot

Superwoman. Shirley Conran. Penguin. 1975.
How to Survive in the Kitchen. Katharine Whitehorn. Eyre Methuen. 1979.
Reader's Digest Household Manual. Hodder and Stoughton. 1977.

6. Working Through Pregnancy

Maternity Rights for Working Women. Jean Coussins. 50p from National Council for Civil Liberties, 186 King's Cross Road, London WC1X 9DE.
Rights for Women. Patricia Hewitt. 85p from National Council for Civil Liberties.
Claim maternity benefit on form BM4 from your local social security office.
Read National Insurance leaflet NI 17A also from your local social security office, Citizens Advice Bureau or post office.

6. Looking After the Under-fives

Nurseries Now. Martin Hughes, Berry Mayall, Peter Moss, Jane Perry, Pat Petrie, Gill Pinkerton. Penguin. 1980.
All Our Children. J. Tizard, P. Moss, J. Perry. Temple Smith. 1976.
Early Experience: Myth and Evidence. A. M. and A. D. B. Clarke. Open Books. 1976.
A Survey of Child Care for Pre-School Children with Working Parents. Peter Mottershead. Equal Opportunities Commission. Overseas House. Quay Street, Manchester M3 3HN. 1978.
Services for Young Children with Working Mothers. Central Policy Review Staff. HMSO. 1978.
Childminder. Brian and Sonia Jackson. Routledge and Kegan Paul. 1979.
Alternative models of group child care for pre-School children of working parents. Peter Moss. Equal Opportunities Commission. 1978.
TUC Charter on Facilities for the Under Fives. Trades Union Congress, Great Russell Street, London WC2. 1978.
Low Cost Day Care Provision for the Under Fives. Department of Health and Social Security. HMSO. 1976.
I want to Work but What About the Kids? Equal Opportunities Commission. 1978.

ADDRESSES

National Childminding Association, Office No. 1., 13 London Road, Bromley, Kent.

National Nursery Education Board, 13 Grosvenor Place, London SW1 7EN.

The Lady, 39–40 Bedford Street, Strand, London WC2E 9ER.

Nursery World. Cliffords Inn, Fetter Lane, London EC4A 1PJ.

Pre-School Playgroups Association, Alford House, Aveline Street, London SE11.

For Nanny and au-pair agencies, see address list for Chapter Fifteen (Crisis).

8. Looking After School Children

Day Care for School Age Children. Robin Simpson. Equal Opportunities Commission. 1978.

9. Self-help Day Care

Self Help Day Care. Julie Kaufmann. 95p from Gingerbread, 35 Wellington Street, London WC1.

Not so Much a Nursery. 20p from Market Nursery, 65 Broke Road, London E8. 01 254 1634.

The Do-It-Yourself Nursery. 50p from London Nursery Campaign, 11 Trendell House, Dod Street, London E14.

Workplace Nurseries – the Why and How. National Union of Journalists, Acorn House, 324–330 Gray's Inn Road, London WC1X 5DP. 30p plus 12p postage.

Workplace Nurseries: a negotiating kit. National Association of Local Government Officers, 1 Mabledon Place, London WC1H 9AT.

Standards of Accommodation and Care in Day Nurseries; Guidelines. Department of Health and Social Security, Alexander Fleming House, Elephant and Castle, London SE1.

At Work Together. Pre-School Playgroups Association. Alford House, Aveline Street, London SE11.

Out of School – Who Cares? Sonia Jackson. Bristol Council for Voluntary Service, 9 Elmdale Road, Tyndall's Park, Bristol.

Holiday Play Schemes. Scottish Community Education Centre, 4 Queen's Ferry Street, Edinburgh EH2 4PA (50p).

Gingerbread Corner. Free (with stamped, self-addressed envelope) from Gingerbread Corner, 21 Fairfield Road, Croydon, Surrey.

Holiday Play Scheme Kit, and Suggestions for Planning a Holiday Playscheme. Free from National Playing Fields Association, 25 Ovington Square, London SW3 1LQ.

Why Lock up Our Schools? £1, and *Action Guide on Applying to Use a School as a Community Resource.* 35p, both from Fair Play for Children, 248 Kentish Town Road, London NW5.

The Directory of Grant Making Trusts. Charity Aid Foundation. (Available in your local library.)

Fund Raising. Hilary Blume. Routledge and Kegan Paul.

Raising Money from Trusts, Raising Money from Government, Raising Money from Industry, Raising Money Through Special Events. £1.05 each plus 25p postage from the Directory of Social Change, 9 Mansfield Place, London NW3.

10. Getting Ready to Jump

Equal Opportunities: A Careers Guide for Women and Men. Ruth Miller. Penguin.

Late Start: Careers for Wives. Penelope Labovitch and Rosemary Simon. New English Library.

Fresh Start. Published jointly by the Equal Opportunities Commission and the National Council for One Parent Families, 255 Kentish Town Road, London NW5.

Handbook of Free Careers Information in the UK. (Lists free careers material available from over 200 professional bodies and training boards with names, addresses and telephone numbers.) £3.00 plus 90p postage from Careers Consultants Ltd, 12–14 Hill Rise, Richmond, Surrey.

Directory of Further Education. Careers Research Advisory Council. In your local library.

Directory of Degree Courses. Free from National Academic Awards, 344–354 Gray's Inn Road, London WC1X 8BP.

How to Apply for Admission to a University. 50p from Universities Central Council on Admissions, Box 28, Cheltenham, Gloucestershire.

Grants to Students: a Brief Guide. Department of Education and Science, Elizabeth House, York Road, London SE1.

Second Chance Education. Ruth Miller. A *Good Housekeeping* Editorial Bulletin, 60p from *Good Housekeeping*, Broadwick House, Broadwick Street, London W1.

Returners. 85p from National Advisory Centre on Careers for Women, 251 Brompton Road, London SW3 2HB.

Her Majesty's Stationery Office publish a wide variety of career guides. To find out if there is one which interests you, write to the HMSO Bookshop, High Holborn, London WC1.

ADDRESSES

Higher Education Advisory Centre, 114 Chase Side, Southgate, London N14 5PN.

National Advisory Centre on Careers for Women, 251 Brompton Road, London SW3 2HB.

Manpower Services Commission (Training Opportunities Scheme), Selkirk House, High Holborn, London WC2.

For information about TOPS courses, contact your local Job Centre or employment office.

The Open University, PO Box 48, Milton Keynes, MK7 6AB.

Independent Assessment and Research Centre, 57 Marylebone High Street, London W1M 3AE.

Vocational Guidance Association, Harley House, Upper Harley Street, London NW1.

The Vocational Guidance Centre, Room 4, Exchange Hall, Corn Exchange Buildings, Hanging Ditch, Manchester M4 3EY.

Careers Research and Advisory Centre (CRAC), Bateman Street, Cambridge CB2 1LZ.

Professional and Executive Recruitment, 4–5 Grosvenor Place, London SW1 7SB.

Educational Grants Advisory Service, 26 Bedford Square, London WC1H 0DN.

Scottish Education Department, New St Andrew's House, St James' Centre, Edinburgh EH1 3SY.

National Union of Students Grants Adviser, 3 Endsleigh Street, London WC1.

Advisory Centre for Education, 18 Victoria Park Square, Bethnal Green, London EC2 9PB.

11. Mothers Versus Employers

The Equality Report. Jean Coussins. £1 from National Council for Civil Liberties.

The Unequal Breadwinner. Ruth Lister and Leo Wilson. 35p from National Council for Civil Liberties.

12. Being Your Own Boss

Home Working. A TUC Statement. 35p from Trades Union Congress, Congress House, Great Russell Street, London WC1.

Starting a Manufacturing Business. John Collins. Small Firms Information Service booklet No. 8. HMSO.

Earning Money At Home. Consumers Association. 14 Buckingham Street, London WC2N 6DS.

Guide to Spare Time Earning. Good Housekeeping Editorial Bulletin. 45p from *Good Housekeeping*, Broadwick House, Broadwick Street, London W1.

ADDRESSES

Small Firms Information Service, Department of Industry, Abell House, John Islip Street, London SW1P 4LN.

13. Mothers and Money

Tax and Sex Discrimination. Patricia Hewitt. 85p from National Council for Civil Liberties.
The Equality Report. John Coussins. £1 from National Council for Civil Liberties.
Inland Revenue Booklets, available from your local tax office:
IR 22. Personal Allowances.
IR 13. Wife's Earnings Election.
IR 31. Income Tax and Married Couples.
IR 29. Income Tax and One Parent Families.
IR 30. Income Tax, Separation and Divorce.
IR 28. Starting in Business.
National Insurance leaflets, available from your local social security office or post office:
NI 27A Self-employed People with Small Earnings.
NI 1. National Insurance Guide for Married Women.
NI 95. Guidance for Women whose marriage is ended by Divorce or Annulment.
NI 196. Benefit Rates.
NI 208. Contribution Rates.

14. One Parent Families

One Parent Families. Edited by Dulan Barber. Teach Yourself Books. Hodder and Stoughton. 1978.
One Parent Families. Diana Davenport. Pan. 1979.
Splitting Up. Catherine Itzin. Virago. 1980.
Mothers Alone. Dennis Marsden. Penguin. 1973.

ADDRESSES

Child Poverty Action Group, 1 Maklin Street, London WC2 5NH.
National Council for One Parent Families, 255 Kentish Town Road, London NW5 2LX.
Gingerbread, 35 Wellington Street, London WC2. 01 240 0953.
Singlehanded Ltd, 68 Lewes Road, Haywards Heath, Sussex.

15. Crisis

SOURCES OF PAID HELP

Brompton Bureau, 10 Beauchamp Place, Knightsbridge, London SW3. 01 584 6242.

Problem Ltd, 179 Vauxhall Bridge Road, London SW1. 01 828 8181. (But you must be a member. Current annual subscription is £25.)

Country Cousins, 98 Billingshurst Road, Broadbridge Heath, Horsham, West Sussex RH12 3LF. Horsham 5188/61960.

Universal Aunts Ltd, 36 Walpole Street, London SW3. 01 730 9834.

Consultus Ltd, 17 London Road, Tonbridge, Kent. Tonbridge 355231.

Babysitters Unlimited, 313 Brompton Road, London SW3. 01 584 0161 or 01 730 7777/8.

Childminders, 67 Marylebone High Street, London W1. 01 935 2049.

The Nanny Service, Oldbury Place, London W1. 01 935 3515.

Au Pair Bureau (Piccadilly) Ltd, 87 Regent Street, London W1. 01 930 4757 or 01 437 6424.

Au Pair Domestic Bureau. Jacey Gall, 523 Oxford Street, London W1. 01 408 1013.

CURRENT ACTION REGISTER OF PARENTS' HELP LINES, COMPILED BY THE NATIONAL CHILDREN'S CENTRE – LONGROYD BRIDGE, HUDDERSFIELD, WEST YORKSHIRE. 0484 41733.
(Contact them for the most up-to-date information on parents' helplines.)

Altrincham, Family Contact Line. 061 941 1155.

Ashton under Lyne. Dial-for-Help. 01 339 2345.

Barnsley. Parents' Action Line. Barnsley 46591.

Belfast. Parents' Advice Centre. Belfast 22227.

Bexley. Parents Anonymous. Erith 31948.

Birmingham. Parents Anonymous. 021 440 5444.

Brighton. Parent Child Concern. Brighton 33012.

Bristol. Parent Child Crisis. Bristol 681907. 832380. 713784. 632409. 559600.

Coventry. Parents Anonymous. 0203 453522.

Crawley. Parents Anonymous. Faygate 534.

Croydon and Tandridge. Parents Anonymous. 01 668 4805.

East Ham. Family Care Unit. 01 471 6569.

Eaton Socon. Walk-in Centre. Huntingdon 216136.

Glasgow. Help a Mum. 041 248 3075.
  C.A.R.E. 041 634 5957 or 634 4476.

Guildford and Cranleigh. Parents Anonymous. 04866 6704.

Harlow. Helpline. Harlow 38010.

Hayes. Hayes Family Group. 01 462 7609.

Hornchurch. Parents Anonymous. Hornchurch 51538. 55001.

Huddersfield. Hotline. 0484 41733.

Leeds. Family Distress Line. 0532 654296.

Leicester. Parents Anonymous. 0533 886735.

Lichfield. Parents Anonymous. Shenstone 480618.

163

Liverpool. Family Link. 051 428 2600.
Newham. Newham Mental Health Project. 01 555 9049.
Northampton. Family Friends. 0604 408305.
Northwood. Parents Anonymous. 65 23483.
Nottingham. Parents Anonymous. 0602 624499.
Ormskirk. Family Aid. Ormskirk 77091.
Oxford. Parents Anonymous. 0865 68901.
Penarth. Parents Helpline. Penarth 705986.
Sheffield. Parents Lifeline. Sheffield 51234.
Southampton. Scope. West End 3680.
Sutton. Parents Anonymous. 01 669 8900.
Swansea. Parents Helpline. 0792 892760.
Tonbridge. Parents S.O.S. Paddock Wood 3318.
Wandsworth. Pre-School Playgroups Association. 01 672 0804 or 01 769 7600.
Wakefield. Help at Hand. 98 65255.
Warrington. Family Distress Service. Warrington 62514.
North Watford. Network. 0923 37010 or 37731.

National Children's Homes run 13 Family Network Centres nationwide. Their central number is 01 226 2033.

16. Parents and Social Security

Social security leaflets; available from your local social security office or post office.
CH11. Child Benefit Increase.
CB1. Child Benefit.
FB1. Family Benefits and Pensions.
NI1. National Insurance Guide for Married Women.
NI 12. Unemployment Benefit.
NI 16. Sickness Benefit.
SB 1. Cash Help – how to claim supplementary benefit.
FIS 1. Family Income Supplement.

17. Working Together

See general reading list.
Other information supplied by individual embassies.

Index